JAY YELAS

A Champion's Journey
of Faith, Family, and Fishing

Published by Cool Springs Press,
a Division of Thomas Nelson, Inc.,
P.O. Box 141000, Nashville, Tennessee, 37214

Library of Congress Cataloging-in-Publication Data

Yelas, Jay A., 1965-
Jay Yelas : a champion's journey of faith, family, and fishing : an autobiography / by Jay Yelas.
p. cm.
ISBN 1-59186-036-9 (pbk. : alk. paper)
1. Yelas, Jay A., 1965- 2. Fishers–United States–Biography. 3. Bass fishing. I. Title.
SH415.Y46A3 2003
799.1'092–dc21

2003000511

First printing 2003
Printed in the United States of America
10 9 8 7 6 5 4 3 2 1

Editor: Ramona D. Wilkes
Editorial Assistance: Mary Ann Lackland of Fluency Organization
Production/Design: Gary Bozeman of Bozeman Design

Photos provided courtesy of:

FLW Outdoors, photography by Yasutaka Ogasawara:
Color insert pages: 8, 9

Mike Walker & The Walker Agency:
Pages: 174
Color insert pages: 11 (bottom), 12 (top), 13 (top), 14, 15, 16
Pure Fishing, Inc.:
Front cover inset
B.A.S.S.
Front and back cover
Inside Pages: 136, 177, 178, 181
Color insert pages: 10, 11 (top), 12 (bottom), 13 (bottom)

All other photos provided by Jay Yelas.

JAY YELAS

A Champion's Journey
of Faith, Family, and Fishing

An Autobiography
By
Jay Yelas

COOL SPRINGS PRESS

Nashville, Tennessee
A Division of Thomas Nelson, Inc.
www.ThomasNelson.com

TABLE OF CONTENTS

DEDICATION

I would like to dedicate this book to the loving memory of my mother-in-law, Joyce Montgomery. Her devout faith and fervent prayers had more of an influence on my conversion to Christianity than anyone or anything else. She almost single-handedly stood in the gap and prayed Jill and me into God's kingdom. I soon caught her contagious faith, and it opened the door to where I am today.

Joyce was a loving, timid, and quiet person, and yet she was a stalwart spiritual warrior. God used her as the single largest influence on molding my faith, and He has since used me to share the Gospel of Jesus Christ with thousands of fishermen across America. Never underestimate the power of a praying grandma!

ACKNOWLEDGEMENTS

Special thanks to my wife, Jill, and my daughters, Hannah and Bethany for their loving patience while I took precious time away from them to write this book.

Also a special thanks is due to my good friend Kelly Jordon who was instrumental in helping to make this book a reality.

INTRODUCTION

A capacity-crowd of bass fans in the Birmingham-Jefferson Civic Center rose to its feet and cheered me on as I took my victory lap at the 2002 CITGO® BASSMASTERS Classic®. It was everything I ever dreamed it would be—cheering fans draped in ticker tape, the American flag over my shoulder, familiar faces of friends and fellow pros, and my wife and kids beside me soaking it in as the ESPN cameras captured it all on national television. Only this was no dream. It was real. After fifteen years of toiling as a pro, I was finally the World Champion in professional bass fishing.

World Champion. That's a pretty weighty title. Nearly everyone dreams of being the best in the world. Though many aspire to the lofty goal of being number one in a chosen field, few have the ability to do what it takes to succeed in a competitive business. Fewer still end up actually achieving their dreams. By the grace of God, I won the World Championship of professional bass fishing, the BASSMASTERS Classic, as well as the 2002 WAL★MART® FLW Tour Angler of the Year title. My childhood dream had become a reality—I was the World Champion, the best fisherman in the land.

My story is one of God-given talent, burning passion, hard work, and a strong Christian faith—the same values and ideals shared by many of the men and women who made this country great. I am so thankful I live in a country where I am free to chase the American dream and capture it in my hands. In America, men and women can accomplish things few people in history have had the liberty to do. In America, the human spirit is free! Mine is a rare story, but it is not a unique one. I've learned there is no end to what we can accomplish, no limits to what we can achieve. The only thing holding us back is the size of our dreams.

As a youth, the success of other world champions in various parts of society inspired me—athletes, business people, public servants. Like them, I dreamed large, I worked hard, and I was driven wildly to live my own version of the American dream as a top bass pro. The examples of other world champions seemed to prove I could reach my goals on my own sweat and toil. I bought into that "make it happen yourself" mentality. I was totally self-centered, focusing exclusively on my dream of being a top bass pro. For years, I tried hard but was unsuccessful at reaching my potential and realizing my dream. I didn't understand that an essential ingredient was missing from the equation for success.

As young adults, we don't often have the wisdom or maturity to see the big picture. Someone has to show it to us. I discovered the missing ingredient in my life was a personal relationship with Jesus Christ. That realization, coupled with a firm decision to begin a relationship with him, changed my life forever. Instantly, things began to click for me. I started getting my priorities in order, which led to a balanced life. I discovered there are more important things in life than winning acclaim for ourselves. My focus shifted from looking out for myself to helping others. Leaving a legacy as the best fisherman in the world was no longer as appealing as leaving a legacy of making the world a better place. My grand love affair with God ushered in a new era in my life. I started living and fishing for His glory, not my own.

What happens to your dream when God comes into the picture? He makes the dream complete. He makes your other relationships complete. A relationship with God makes your entire life complete. By living the dream God gave me and having a platform as a champion fisherman, I have the opportunity to help other people and make the world a better place. I believe the best way I can do this is to share the truth of God's word. Looking back now, my dream was just a foundation for God to use me to have a much greater impact on the world than just winning fishing tournaments. I had to grow as a champion in life long before I was able to gain the title of World Champion in bass fishing.

Winning the 2002 Classic was a tremendous honor! The field was stacked with the most talented fishermen in the world, many of whom are much more talented than I am. However, it was my turn. I believe when the Lord decides it is your turn— you win. It's that simple. "With God, all things are possible," (Matthew 19:26).

The Keys to My Success

Looking back over my fifteen years as a professional bass fisherman, I have pinpointed some recurring lessons that have been the "keys" to my success in fishing and in life. I learned some of these lessons the hard way (from my mistakes) and others just from being observant and open-minded.

Many things are woven into our lives that influence us and guide us, but for this book I have narrowed these influences—or keys—down to seven subjects. You will see examples of these subjects highlighted throughout the book with a directional icon, indicating a life lesson learned as a result of that key influence.

Of course, God influences me in ALL things. I have not tried to mark every instance where God has affected my life—I could have covered each page with examples! God had a plan for me, and these keys helped me to live up to that plan. It's my hope that you will find some examples in my keys to success that you can relate to your own life.

Key Symbol:

1. **Family** (importance of encouragement, support, comfort)
2. **Focus** (importance of the power of a dream, determination, sacrifice)
3. **Mentoring** (importance of teaching, leading and living by example, accountability)
4. **Giving** (importance of time, talents, financial resources)
5. **Work Ethic** (importance of earning income, learning responsibility)
6. **Patience** (importance of timing, rewards, peace)
7. **Courage** (importance of persistence, facing change)

SECTION ONE:
INFLUENCE

Son, doing 'good' is not good enough for you.
You're capable of being great.
Nothing in this world can hold you back.

—My uncle, Bill Yelas, encouraging me as a youth.

Chapter One

BORN TO FISH

Some might say my childhood was a dream, growing up on the water in a suburb of Honolulu, Hawaii, until the age of twelve. As a boy, I spent a lot of time playing in my backyard—only my backyard was a bay in Hawaii Kai. Some of my earliest memories are of days spent water-skiing behind our family's 33-horsepower tri-hull boat in the beautiful clear bay and the sharp sting of the salty warm ocean water splashing my face. An occasional stingray or even a small shark would come into view below. Other times, my dad and I would trek down to our dock and motor out through the lagoon to fish beyond the reef where the bay spilled into the Pacific Ocean. We used dead shrimp to try to get something to bite. On more than one occasion, we were on the lookout for the Hawaii state fish, the humuhumunukunukuapuaa. It's a mouthful no matter how you pronounce it, but I'm proud to say I've caught that fish!

My best buddy through grade school, Tony Arnone, and I would untie my canoe and paddle in and out of coves in the bay, spending endless days fishing for perch from the canoe. Our house had a rock retaining wall off the water's edge—a perfect place to catch crabs. My friends and I loved to bait our crab rings with dead fish, throw them out in the lagoon, and catch the crabs. We'd throw them back or bring these Hawaiian crabs home to our families if they were big enough to eat. Hawaii was and still is a young boy's paradise.

I was lucky, as were all my childhood friends, to live in a part of the country that afforded a young boy so many avenues to experience nature. Like all kids, we took advantage of every opportunity to play outdoors and "take it all in." At the start of one summer, we came up with an idea for a research project. We used a felt tip marker to identify the crabs we caught by writing a small number on their shells. Then we recorded the date and threw them back into the water. All summer long, we tried to recapture those same crabs, recording our results each day in a water-stained notebook we kept with us.

It's in the Genes

I'm often asked if the affinity for fishing runs in the family. My dad liked to fish when he was a boy with his brother and dad, a hobby that continued into his adult years. My dad didn't have an

My dad's parents had a summer cabin in upstate New York on Lake Ontario. Dad was the first person I ever went fishing with, and here we are at Sandy Pond, our favorite spot.

Here I am, the happiest two-year-old in the world, proudly holding my first fish—a blue gill ("Rock Bass" they call them up north) that Dad and I caught together.

unusual passion for fishing, but he did have a drive and determination to succeed. My dad, Joe Yelas, grew up on the East Coast and attended Hobart College in New York. He was an education major with aspirations of one day being an administrator in private education. When he met my mom, Kim Griffiths, she was studying education at an all-girls college, William-Smith, preparing to be a kindergarten teacher. They fell in love and married. As young college graduates with no real commitments weighing them down, my parents decided Hawaii would be an ideal place to live and work. My dad and mom took jobs at Iolani, a private college preparatory school for K-12 in Honolulu. My mom became a kindergarten

Some might say my childhood was a dream, growing up in a suburb of Honolulu, Hawaii. When I wasn't on the water, you could find me on the field, playing T-ball and other sports.

teacher at Iolani, a profession she faithfully and wholeheartedly served for thirty years. My dad began the slow climb up the administrative ladder and accepted a position as a high school math teacher and football coach.

I was born Joel Andrew Yelas on September 2, 1965, in Honolulu, five or six years after my mom and dad first moved to Hawaii. What my parents originally chose as a good biblical name was eventually shortened to Jay. Since our parents were both faculty members at Iolani—an academic powerhouse—my younger sister, Lisa, and I received the benefit of a first-rate, high-priced education free of charge. As you can imagine, education was big around my house, but I admit I didn't make straight A's. I had my share of A's from time to time, but I also had my share of C's, although I was a B-student on average. My favorite subject was math, and I still have an aptitude for numbers.

My dad played college football and baseball at Hobart, so there was no shortage of sports enthusiasts around our house. I played every sport a young boy could get into in those days—tee ball and later baseball, football, and basketball. I loved the water, but my buddies and I were just as active off the water as we were on it. My mom and dad went to all my games, faithfully cheering me on as I rounded the bases or made a 3-pointer on the basketball court. Dad spent lots of time with me as a young boy, shooting hoops and pitching to me for batting practice in the front yard until his arm was so sore it just hung at his side like a piece of meat.

Family

At Taft Dock, I was happy even when it was just the water, the fish, and me.

Moving On

My dad became Assistant Headmaster at Iolani, reaping the reward for his steadfast determination and hard work. After fifteen years of service at Iolani, he earned a sabbatical at the start of my fifth grade year. My family packed up and moved all the way to the northeast, close to my dad's family near Hartford, Connecticut. We stayed there for the next year. We traded our swimsuits for snowsuits—man was it cold! I remember blowing into my hands to keep them warm at New York Mets baseball games with my dad and watching the Jets play football in the snow as the fans shivered in the stands. We fished on the Podunk River, catching catfish for the most part, along with bass, bluegills, and whatever else would bite. What we call brim back in Texas, the northeasterners call "pumpkin seeds," and these little guys proved to be an easy catch.

No doubt, Connecticut was very different from Hawaii Kai,

My paternal grandfather, Joe Yelas, taking my sister and me fishing in his boat on Sandy Pond in upstate New York.

but I liked the change. The kids at Wapping Elementary School in South Windsor thought my Hawaiian accent sounded cool! Back home in Hawaii I was the minority among all the Oriental and Hawaiian students, but I didn't know the difference. Now for the first time in my life, I looked like everyone else—or they looked like me!

After we returned to Hawaii I made the freshman basketball team even though I was only in the seventh grade. I was a good athlete, but the other players thought it was a sham. This was my first taste of racial tension. The kids thought of me as the privileged "white boy" and said my dad's role as Assistant Headmaster was the only reason I made the team. Like any child, I had my fair share of kids trying to start something with me after school, chasing me around on the playground. At the end of that school year my dad was offered a Headmaster position in Phoenix, Arizona, and I was ready to move on.

I HAD MY FAIR SHARE OF KIDS TRYING TO START SOMETHING WITH ME AFTER SCHOOL, CHASING ME AROUND ON THE PLAYGROUND. AT THE END OF THAT YEAR, I WAS READY TO MOVE ON.

Moving to Phoenix brought me one step closer to my destiny. For eighth-grade I attended my dad's school, All Saints Episcopal Day School, and transferred to Sunnyslope High School my freshman year where I played junior varsity baseball, among other sports. After an outstanding season at "Slope" where our football team went undefeated all year, my dad received yet another offer to be Headmaster, this time for a K-12 private school in Santa Barbara, California. However, my dad decided to leave that job mid-year, so I transferred to San Marcos High School in Santa Barbara halfway through my tenth-grade year where I stayed through graduation.

I ended up attending six different schools between kindergarten and high school graduation, including five schools between seventh-grade and tenth-grade. I know moving to new schools and starting over is difficult for many kids, but I learned

I THREW OUT A

BLACK JITTERBUG

AND BEGAN REELING

IT IN. WHEN A

13-INCH BASS TOOK

THE BAIT, I

THOUGHT I WOULD

BUST WITH

EXCITEMENT! THAT

WAS THE FIRST

BASS I CAUGHT ON

MY OWN.

to roll with the punches, making new friends and scouting out what new sports teams these schools had to offer. Moving was a pain, sure, but I can't complain too much since we did live in some of the most beautiful climates in the country.

Moving from city to city and school to school prepared me for a similar lifestyle as a pro bass fisherman. My parents' openness to new experiences had an influence on me that I know helped shape my life. These days I am sometimes in ten or more different cities in a month's time, working and speaking at various events. My job requires that I often work outside my comfort zone, and I firmly believe my parents' adventurous nature, combined with my moves during my youth, prepared me to learn how to meet new people and adjust to new situations. What do you expect from a guy whose newlywed parents moved on a whim to the island state of Hawaii just because it sounded fun?

Family Inheritance

Dad was the first person I ever went fishing with. We had some fabulous times as a family each summer, visiting his parents in upstate New York. My dad's parents had a summer cabin at Sandy Pond. We water-skied and fished for bass in the evening in a bay connected to the deep blue waters of Lake Ontario. I was the happiest two-year old in the world, proudly holding the blue gill (called "Rock Bass" up north) that he and I caught together. One morning when I was eight or nine years old, standing alone down on the dock of my grandfather's cabin, I threw out a black jitterbug and began reeling it in, working it

The Yelas family returns from a salmon fishing-charter out of Depoe Bay in Oregon.

slowly on the surface. When a 13-inch bass took the bait, I thought I would bust with excitement! That was the first bass I caught on my own. I didn't catch another bass until I fished on Lake Cachuma in high school many years later.

We spent most of every summer with my mom's parents in Lincoln City, Oregon. The Oregon coast is teeming with outdoor recreational opportunities. I absolutely loved being there. We played in the woods, fished the ocean, rivers and lakes, crabbed, hiked, picked blackberries and played on the beach. My sister Lisa loved to fish almost as much as I did. Our favorite spot as youngsters was Taft Dock, a public fishing pier in the Siletz Bay. Lisa and I would fish all summer, keeping track

The Oregon coast offers many outdoor activities. My sister, Lisa, and I played in the woods, crabbed, hiked, picked blackberries, played on the beach, and fished at our favorite spot, Taft Dock in the Siletz Bay.

of our catch in a contest to see who could rack up the most fish. One summer, it was a pretty close call with her total reaching 345 perch and mine just beating her at 379! From an early age, when I went fishing or crab hunting, Lisa was right there with me. She's still a pretty good hand at fishing herself and loves the outdoors.

Family

Taft Dock was the backdrop for many of my boyhood memories. Many mornings during the summer my Mom would take me to the dock, drop me off on her way to Salem (about 60 miles away), and return for me at dinnertime. I'd love it! Just the water, the fish, and me. When my parents couldn't give me a ride to Taft Dock, I would walk to the beach and follow it south about a mile and a half to the dock, despite lugging my 10-pound crab ring and my fishing rod. At the end of the day, I'd haul it all with me back to the house. Dad would also take me trolling in the Siletz River for blueback, a sea-run cutthroat trout that spends most of its adult life in the ocean.

When I was five years old, I recall my maternal grandfather, the Reverend Alfred Griffiths, taking me on a chartered salmon fishing trip out of Depoe Bay in Oregon. Six people, including my grandfather and me, trolled all morning and caught two salmon. Grandpa and I didn't catch any that day, but what a thrill it was being with my grandfather out on the water! I recall him also taking me for yellow perch, flounder, and bullheads on Taft Dock. My tiny hands got lost in his, which were wrinkled with age. He died the following year, but I'll always have fond memories of fishing with him.

MY MOM WOULD TAKE ME TO THE DOCK, DROP ME OFF ON HER WAY TO SALEM, AND RETURN FOR ME AT DINNERTIME. I'D LOVE IT! JUST THE WATER, THE FISH, AND ME.

Unlike my love for the outdoors and the natural draw I had for sports and fishing, the spiritual side of who I was didn't receive the same nurturing and encouragement. Growing up in the church, I learned various Bible stories in Sunday school. I even remember there was something about the church experience I liked as a young boy—I just didn't know what it was that drew my interest. The church did what it could to teach me, but I wasn't making the connection, and eventually that interest faded over time.

I distinctly recall attending a church camp on one of the outer islands of Hawaii as a grade-school boy and feeling receptive and open to spiritual things as the leader talked to us boys around a campfire. However, it would be twenty years before I heard a similar message of God's love and or understood what he had done for me so I could love him in return.

The Importance of Influence

Even with these fun-filled summer excursions, I still spent more time playing team sports as a kid than fishing. I cannot necessarily look back and identify the single influence on my life that made me who I am today. Whatever is encouraged in a child eventually surfaces. My parents encouraged me to try new

Family

things; they didn't push me in one direction or the other. They faithfully exposed me to a variety of sports and activities and provided an ideal setting for me to discover my gifts and talents. Encouragement is an environment—a combination of people, places, and things that shape us into the people we are. And those results can be positive or negative.

The vote of confidence I most remember really came from my Uncle Bill—my dad's younger brother and one of my personal heroes as a child. A sports enthusiast who played baseball in college, not to mention the fact that he was an excellent golfer, told me I could do anything I wanted with my life. I recall one day coming home from school and my uncle asking about how I did in some sporting event that day. My dad said I did well, but Uncle Bill was quick to respond, "Son, doing 'good' is not good enough for you. You're capable of being great. You can do anything you set your mind to do. You're very gifted, Jay, and nothing in this world can hold you back."

THESE TIMES WE SPENT TOGETHER AS A FAMILY GAVE ME A LOVE OF SPORTS AND THE OUTDOORS. THIS LOVE IS THE FOUNDATION FOR ALL THE DECISIONS THAT BROUGHT ME TO THE PLACE I AM TODAY.

My wife, Jill, and I always make a point to say positive things to our children each day. We also "bless" them by telling them they are gifted and talented, smart and pretty. We tell them they're well-mannered, obedient little girls who have great respect for adults so that they will learn to grow into that expectation. We must discipline them from time to time, but we do it out of love. I always go back and explain why I had to discipline them. Parenthood is an incredibly influential role—one I don't take lightly as I see the influence my dad and mom have had on my life.

My parents always made my sister and me feel like we were their top priority. I admire my mom for her uncanny ability to round up our active family for a sit-down dinner together every night. On special nights, my family and I would pile into the family boat in Honolulu just as the sun was setting off the bay and motor over to a restaurant across the lagoon for dinner.

We took a lot of camping trips from our Oregon summer home to places like the Redwood National Forest in California and Banff National Park in Canada. Those were some of the highlights of my younger days, and I'm glad to say these times we spent together as a family gave me a love of sports and the outdoors. This love is the foundation for all the decisions that brought me to the place I am today.

"The Lakes Are Turning Green"

—Headline in a *Los Angeles Times* article
on the lucrative business of being a successful pro angler,
spring 1983.

Chapter Two

Hooked on Bass

High School Days

In the summer of 1980, my family moved to Santa Barbara, California, after my freshman year of high school in Phoenix. I was oblivious to it then, but for the first time in my life, I was moving to a place where bass fishing was readily accessible to me. Call it divine intervention. Growing up in Honolulu and then Phoenix, I had a hard time getting into the bass fishing scene. There just wasn't enough bass (or "little green trout") in those places.

Santa Barbara isn't exactly the bass capital of the world either, but it was a short thirty minutes away from the Santa Ynez river valley, the home of Lake Cachuma—the only reservoir within a one and a half hour drive of Santa Barbara. Granted, Cachuma is a small lake (only 3,250 acres), but at least it was a good lake with some nice bass in it. If it weren't for Lake Cachuma, I don't know if I would have gotten involved in bass fishing.

In the winter of 1982, my dad decided to buy a boat for us to go fishing together on Lake Cachuma. Being the trout troller he was, he decided all we needed was a 13-foot johnboat powered by a 4-horsepower outboard. I didn't really care. I was so into playing baseball at the time that I didn't have too much interest in going fishing. However, I liked the idea of spending some one-on-one time with Dad.

This little prize pram didn't even have a trailer. We simply left it in a storage yard adjacent to Harvey Bay, a small cove near the dam on Cachuma. Every time we wanted to go fishing, we got the boat out of storage and carried it down a steep hill to the water. Then we walked back up the hill, got the engine, gas tank, and all our tackle out of the trunk of the car, and carried them down to the boat. As a high school principal, Dad favored his conservative Oldsmobile sedan over a more fishing-friendly truck or Suburban, so we always had to carry the rods inside the car with us. When we pulled up to the lake, I'm sure we must have looked like some city slicker goobers without a clue!

In all fairness to Dad, there were more than a few luxury sedans in the parking lot at Lake Cachuma every weekend. Nestled between the Coastal Mountain range and the San Rafael Mountains, it was the fishing destination of some of the most refined anglers without a fly rod I've ever seen. Anglers like us, fresh off the beach in Santa Barbara and toting rods inside the car for a day of trout fishing—this was the norm around Cachuma. Santa Barbara is a very well-to-do community, and

Brad Sharpton was the only kid in my high school who was more interested in fishing than the nearby sun and surf, so we naturally gravitated to one another. Brad played baseball with more intensity than any other kid on our team did, and I admired his competitive edge, too. Later, we were roommates at Oregon State.

Dad and I couldn't have guessed I would one day point to Lake Cachuma as the starting place of my bass fishing career.

When I wasn't on Lake Cachuma, a fishing buddy and I were hitting the few ponds in town that were loaded with bass. We especially liked the pond on the fourteenth hole at Le Cumbre Country Club! The golfers let us fish there when they were done for the day. Man, what a gold mine that place was!

I didn't start out chasing bass. No, as a high school student the wily hatchery trout had my attention. When we started fishing, my dad wanted to troll for trout and I was just along for a good time, so I followed his lead. Cachuma is stocked with hatchery trout every winter, beginning in October. And we caught 'em, filling our limits with ten nice rainbows.

We trolled "about seven colors," letting out about 70 feet of lead-core line that changed color every 10 feet. It was fun catching those trout, but it wasn't a huge challenge or thrill. Reeling in a 12-inch trout with 70 feet of 20-pound line on an elephant gun of a rod isn't exactly sporting. However, it was an acceptable excuse for a fifteen-year-old kid to spend a fun Saturday afternoon with Dad.

Lake Cachuma is a federally owned facility, leased and operated by Santa Barbara County, which manages the drinking water supply for the city of Santa Barbara. There were no private interests on the lake, just one lonely marina run by the county. They operated a fleet of rental boats, sold a smattering of tackle, cooked up breakfast and lunch, and most importantly, weighed and photographed extraordinary stringers of fish caught in the lake. This little corner of the marina at Lake Cachuma set the scene for the next step of my transformation into a competitive fishing monster.

IT WAS FUN CATCHING THOSE TROUT, BUT IT WASN'T A HUGE CHALLENGE OR THRILL. REELING IN A 12-INCH TROUT WITH 70 FEET OF 20-POUND LINE ON AN ELEPHANT GUN OF A ROD ISN'T EXACTLY SPORTING.

Catching On

It seemed I transformed overnight from a happy-go-lucky kid out for a good time with Dad to a fierce competitor. I began to live to out-fish everyone on the lake. I realize now that God made me that way. All I knew then was how much I couldn't stand it when Dad and I came in from a day of mediocre trout fishing and saw other guys weighing in and photographing huge stringers of trout. I burned inside! I vowed to myself and to Dad we could catch more than the other guys the next Saturday.

At the same time, I began to catch on to better ways to catch trout than trolling. I knew the cheese fishermen "waxed" the trollers from time to time with the amount of fish they caught. I talked Dad into buying some Velveeta® cheese the next time out. (Hey, don't laugh, that stuff worked!) We anchored up in the back of Cachuma Bay or behind Arrowhead Island and limited out on the number of fish we could catch in no time. That was back in the days before Berkley® introduced their Trout PowerBait® imitation cheese—if only we'd had that winner back in 1981!

I COULDN'T STAND IT WHEN DAD AND I CAME IN FROM A DAY OF MEDIOCRE TROUT FISHING AND SAW OTHER GUYS WEIGHING IN AND PHOTOGRAPHING HUGE STRINGERS. I BURNED INSIDE!

Less than a year passed before Dad and I started catching fish as well as anybody on that lake. In fact, I really started getting into it. I was beginning to have so much fun that I invited a friend from my baseball team at San Marcos High School to go fishing with me one weekend. My friend, Brad Sharpton, had been telling me his tall tales of fishing with his grandpa on Douglas Lake in Tennessee. He was the only other kid in high school who was more interested in fishing than the nearby sun and surf, so we naturally gravitated to one another. Brad played baseball with more intensity than any other kid on our team did, and I admired his competitive edge, too. He played hard and hated to lose—my kind of guy!

Christmas came early on December 24, 1982! I caught my first 7-pound bass while I was fishing on Lake Cachuma—the only reservoir within a one and a half hour drive of Santa Barbara, California.

We packed up the next Saturday and headed up to Cachuma for some trout fishing. We caught some nice strings of rainbows and really began to enjoy our time fishing together. We started going to Cachuma at every opportunity. Neither of us had time for girls or the high school party scene. In fact, I didn't even go to my senior prom! There was an unbelievable topwater bite going on up at Cachuma that weekend, and I wanted to be on the water at daylight that next Saturday morning. Baseball and fishing were our joint passions—but the day was coming when one of those interests would takeover.

A Humble Beginning

One January day Brad and I were anchored in the back of Cachuma Bay, soaking Velveeta cheeseballs in vain and watching the morning fog quietly lift off the water. The trout were taking the day off. Suddenly the hum of an outboard motor shattered the peaceful morning as a shiny, sleek bass boat slid into our sleepy little cove. Our new guests had my full attention. I watched in awe as the two anglers in their flashy bass rig jumped up, ran to the bow, and threw their trolling motor in the water. Without a sound, they picked up their crankbaits and stood side by side, as they quietly eased down the bank, casting and retrieving, casting and retrieving.

SPELLBOUND, I WIPED THE VELVEETA OFF MY HANDS AND ONTO MY JEANS. I HEARD ONE OF THEM CRY, "GET THE NET!" THEN THE BASS JUMPED!

Spellbound, I wiped the Velveeta off my hands and onto my jeans. I heard one of them cry, "Get the net!" One guy ran for the net as the other went into that instinctive knees-bent, crouched-over position—something I learned to recognize as a sure sign of a good bass. Then the bass jumped! The guy ceremoniously fought it a while longer before his buddy slipped it in the net. They held up a good 4-pound bass and then put it in the livewell. As I reeled in another cheeseball, these conquering heroes took off down the bank, casting and reeling. They caught another crankbait fish, and I twiddled my thumbs, my cheeseball soaking 30 feet below.

Brad piped up with the obvious. "All that casting and reeling and catching fish looks like a heck of a lot more fun than what we're doing," he announced. I agreed, and we vowed to go bass fishing the following Saturday.

The next week after baseball practice, we made a trip over to Santa Barbara's best and only legitimate tackle shop, Hook, Line, and Sinker, to pick up some bass tackle. We looked around the shop a while and settled on two crankbaits. We each bought a Hellbender. Brad's was a greenish frog color, and mine was brown like a crawdad. That was it. We each had a spinning rod we'd been using for trout, and we figured that would do equipment-wise.

Equipped with my Dad's 13-foot johnboat and nothing else, we went bass fishing. When we got to a likely looking bank, one of us rowed while the other one casted. We were a mess! I think each of us hooked the other twice that day. On one memorable cast, my Hellbender caught on Brad's ball cap, and I cast the thing into the lake! I recall Brad had some rather choice words for me. No wonder I was a little paranoid when it became my turn to row again!

Brad and I each caught one bass on that chilly day. I caught the first one, a good-sized beauty that looked to me like it had to weigh over a ton. I can still recall the exact spot I caught that bass, on the river rock shoreline just left of Arrowhead Island, leading into the Narrows (which is the upper river portion of Lake Cachuma). I also recall the distinct thrill of feeling this fish tug on my line. We dug out the stringer from the bottom of the tackle box and strung it up—I was so proud.

Later that day the game warden stopped us, and he took my prize fish to measure it. I didn't even realize there was a minimum size on bass, so I never measured that fish. We just dragged it around on a stringer all day, displaying our catch. That game warden was the first to tell me of the 12-inch minimum on bass in California. I held my breath and waited nervously as he took my bass off the stringer to measure it. It went to 12 inches—but just barely. I look back on that episode now and sometimes wonder what I would have done had that fish been too short. The fine may have

THAT GAME WARDEN WAS THE FIRST TO TELL ME OF THE 12-INCH MINIMUM ON BASS IN CALIFORNIA. I HELD MY BREATH AND WAITED NERVOUSLY AS HE TOOK MY BASS OFF THE STRINGER TO MEASURE IT.

A 45-pound Chinook salmon from the Siletz River—still the biggest fish I've ever caught in my life!

turned me off from bass fishing all together—but I doubt it!

Later that day we headed into the Narrows, and Brad caught a nice three and one-half pounder on his Hellbender off the right hand point of Horse Canyon cove—another indelible moment in life. We were so excited about those fish that we took them right up to the fish cleaning station near the marina to show off our catch.

The fish cleaning station was another place besides the marina boastful anglers took their catch. Competitive juices reached their peak each day at the marina weigh scales or at the fish cleaning station.

Young and old, I guess all anglers are the same. We all get a little envious when someone else catches more than we do.

I never went trout fishing again on that lake. Brad and I turned our focus to bass fishing that day and never looked back. We made two or three more trips with the oars before we splurged and bought a trolling motor and battery. By February of 1982, I was a sixteen-year-old high school junior with a severe case of bass fever.

Bass Fever

In my opinion, high school is way too early to worry about a career as a pro. I don't recommend beginning a pro bass fishing career until after graduating from college.

However, I had a late start compared to many kids I meet in bass fishing circles these days. And mine was a very humble start. I fished out of that 13-foot johnboat all through high school. Yet I meet many high school kids whose parents have provided them with fully rigged fiberglass bass boats. There is nothing wrong with that; it just isn't necessary. That early in life, the only thing that matters for an aspiring bass pro is what is in the heart. If a burning desire is there, that is all someone needs.

I spent my high school days falling in love with the game of bass fishing and soaking up bass fishing information like a sponge. I subscribed to *BASSMASTER® Magazine, U.S. Bass,* and every other bass fishing tabloid I discovered. When each new issue arrived in the mail, I read it cover to cover and then read it over again about twenty times before the next issue arrived. I watched the bass fishing shows on TV as well, but there were not too many of them back in 1982. I recall really enjoying Jerry McKinnis' "Fishin' Hole," and Bill Dance's show. I bought books by Dance, Roland Martin, Rick Clunn, Jimmy Houston, and every other book I could find on the subject. I also recall making a few trips to the library to read up on crawfish, shad, bass, etc.

THE ONLY THING THAT MATTERS FOR AN ASPIRING YOUNG PRO IS WHAT IS IN THE HEART. IF A BURNING DESIRE IS THERE, THAT IS ALL SOMEONE NEEDS.

An aspiring angler's job of learning the sport of bass fishing is easier today. The internet has opened up a new realm for acquiring fishing information. Unlike when I was learning the sport in the 80's, fishing shows abound today, not to mention the countless seminars given by bass pros, or the Pro/Am style tournaments that are so prevalent.

When Brad and I started bass fishing Lake Cachuma, we fished every weekend that spring and summer of '82. Sometimes we even camped at Cachuma overnight. During the week after baseball practice, Brad and I and a few other friends slipped over to Hope Ranch Pond for a little bassin' before dinner. We just used to kill them in that pond. We caught thirty or forty bass in an evening, just fishing off the bank. Having that kind of success really breeds a love for the sport. It is so important for kids who are new to the sport to have fun catching bass. I am so glad I had places to go where I could catch so many fish.

Brad and I became best friends throughout high school and ended up going to college together at Oregon State. I am so thankful I had a best friend to share those early days of fishing. His friendship was also an integral part of my formative years of learning the sport. I doubt I could have maintained my intense drive on my own. There would have been too many lonely days as a kid on the lake without Brad around. Yet as much time as we spent fishing together, eventually my intense drive to master the sport outpaced even Brad's fishing interests. My best bud didn't want to fish every free moment of every day—every weekend! "Go ahead," I encouraged him when he wanted to pass on a fishing trip in order to sleep in, hang out with friends, or go to a game (typical teenager activities). "You're the one who's normal!" We laughed about my obsession. "I'm the one who is abnormally drawn to this fishing thing!"

BRAD AND I AND A FEW OTHER FRIENDS SLIPPED OVER TO HOPE RANCH POND FOR A LITTLE BASSIN' BEFORE DINNER. WE CAUGHT THIRTY OR FORTY IN AN EVENING.

I remember catching my first 7-pounder on Christmas Eve, 1982, on a copper foil Bagley® DB3. That same day, Brad stepped on a rusty nail at the boat dock, and the nail went clean through the sole of his tennis shoes. He had to be rushed to the hospital. I stayed at the lake and pounded them that day. I sure had fun filling him in on what he had missed!

Bill Sedar, owner of Hook, Line and Sinker tackle shop, and my fishing mentor since I was sixteen years old.

Hook, Line and Sinker

Every fisherman I talked to in town said Bill Sedar was the king of Lake Cachuma. No one else even came close. Retired, he had been fishing Cachuma since this man-made lake was filled in 1954. When we met, Bill had been fishing that lake five days a week for twenty-two years—I don't know of anyone who has ever spent more time on one lake! Think of the wisdom he held after bass fishing the same 3,250 acre lake five days a week for over two decades. Bill became a great friend and mentor to me. He took me under his wing and taught me everything he knew. I was blessed with the world's best mentor who just happened to own the best tackle shop in Santa Barbara.

Bill's daughter, Jean Sedar, ran the shop. Brad and I paid her frequent visits and spent most of our hard-earned grass-cutting money on fishing gear. Brad and I were slow learners but "fast accumulators" when it came to fishing tackle. We were good customers. I used to cut a lot of grass for neighbors and do odd landscaping jobs to raise my fishing capital. I spent a few

Work Ethic

31

months working at a gas station, pumping gas and working behind the counter. My typical weekend consisted of working one day and fishing the next day. I had to work or I had no money for fishing.

I still remember buying my first bait casting reel, the Daiwa® PMF 1500. It was the first baitcaster to incorporate a magnetic brake on the spool. It took a while, but I finally got the hang of it. I accumulated a lot of lures, rods, and reels over those early years. Soon I wanted to step up my fish catching to the next level, and I knew I had to have a depthfinder. So I invested in my first major purchase—the yellow box. The "Bird Trap" (as we used to call it) was a portable Humminbird® flasher in a yellow box. I used to stick the transducer over the transom of the boat each time out. A big, black suction cup held the transducer to the boat. In a few short months, I had accumulated a trolling motor, a bunch of terminal tackle, and a sonar unit. I was on my way, baby!

LOOKING BACK, I'M GLAD MY PARENTS DIDN'T GIVE ME WHATEVER I WANTED. IT IS A COMPETITIVE WORLD OUT THERE, AND IF SOMEONE WANTS TO BE SUCCESSFUL, HE OR SHE NEEDS TO LEARN HOW TO WORK HARD.

Looking back, I am glad my parents didn't just give me whatever I wanted. Although I enjoyed many opportunities for travel and education, I wasn't born with a silver spoon in my mouth, that's for sure. My dad could have bought me all the fishing gear I wanted, but he didn't. He knew better. Kids who have to work for what they want learn a strong work ethic. My dad taught me that simple, but very powerful truth at an early age. I think that is the proper way to raise kids, and I plan to do the same with my kids. It is a competitive world out there, and if someone wants to be successful, he or she needs to learn how to work hard. Very hard. That's what the power of a dream is all about.

Steering Toward a Dream

In America, the entrepreneurial spirit is alive and well. We are free to have an idea, a dream, a goal, and to do everything in our power to achieve it. *The Millionaire Next Door,* by Thomas J. Stanley (Longstreet Press, Inc., October 1996), is a great book recounting a survey of hundreds of millionaires to see how they became so wealthy. The findings prove the vast majority of millionaires are self-made. They worked hard to get the most out of their God-given talents and abilities.

Work Ethic

According to the survey, most children of millionaires often end up not doing much with their lives. It turns out, most millionaires spoil their children, giving them everything they want. The children in turn have few accomplishments in their own lives. I never had a car during high school. I rode my bike to school every day. And let me tell you, there were not many seniors in the wealthy community of Santa Barbara, California, who rode bicycles to school. But I didn't mind. It was good exercise, and it kept me humble.

WE NEVER FULLY REALIZE THE POWER OF A DREAM UNTIL AND UNLESS IT IS THE RIGHT DREAM. SOME PEOPLE WORK ALL THEIR LIVES ACHIEVING DREAMS OTHER PEOPLE HAVE FOR THEM.

We never fully realize the power of a dream until and unless it is the right dream. Some people work hard all their lives achieving dreams other people have for them. For example, a son may follow his dad's example and become a lawyer. The son works hard and makes it to the top of his profession. The only problem is law isn't his passion. If he were to pursue his real passion in life, his real dream would take him down a different path altogether--but at the risk of disappointing his father and his family. Therefore, he never knows what it's like to be driven by the power of a dream. He only knows that despite how hard he works, fulfillment seems just beyond his grasp.

Finding My Gift

I tried many sports throughout junior high and as a freshman and sophomore in high school. I played football, basketball, and baseball. I even played in some golf tournaments. But after my sophomore year, I decided to give up playing all the other sports and just concentrate on baseball. It was my favorite, and I guess I was better at it than any other school sport. I played second base, shortstop, and third base. I loved playing the game and still do to this day. I remember spending many nights listening to the Los Angeles Dodgers games on the radio and keeping score of every pitch.

I thought I might have a future in baseball, and I later tried out at Oregon State, but I could see right away I didn't have the physical skills necessary to continue. To be honest, the baseball dream was very easy to give up because I had already found another love that I was better at: bass fishing. When I began fishing it came easily to me, and I was more successful at it than the average person. I was in many competitive arenas, but there was something special about fishing. I sensed I had a gift.

WHEN I BEGAN FISHING IT CAME EASILY TO ME, AND I WAS MORE SUCCESSFUL AT IT THAN THE AVERAGE PERSON. I SENSED I HAD A GIFT.

Don't get me wrong, team sports are great. However, fishing attracted me because it is an individual sport. In fishing, you don't have any teammates, there's no coach; it's you versus the fish. I felt like I didn't have to rely on anyone else but myself. If I did poorly, it wasn't my teammate's fault or my coach's fault. I was solely responsible. I enjoy that aspect of individuality and independence even today.

I believe we are happiest when we are using God-given talents to work hard and fulfill a dream. My love of the outdoors and natural instincts on the water helped me to hone in on what

Focus

I wanted to do with my life. I guess I listened to what my heart was telling me—and I've never regretted it. Needless to say, back in the '80s, my dream of being a bass pro wasn't mainstream. In my day, being a professional bass fisherman was unheard of. All I knew was I couldn't shake the dream—and I was willing to work without a single wasted day in order to see it become reality.

Staying Afloat

High school graduation finally came in 1983. By that time, I was locked in on a career as a pro bass fisherman, even though it was a relatively new professional sport. An article about the money potential in professional bass fishing came out in the *L.A. Times* with the headline, "The Lakes Are Turning Green." I can still remember the look of disbelief on my dad's face when I read the article aloud in our kitchen and told him my career aspirations. "See, Dad? I could make a career out of bass fishing!" To which he quickly responded, "Oh, no, you're not!"

MY DREAM OF BEING A BASS PRO WASN'T MAINSTREAM. IN MY DAY, BEING A PROFESSIONAL BASS FISHERMAN WAS UNHEARD OF.

Since my mom and dad were both educators, the idea of foregoing college was unimaginable. Therefore, my game plan was to get my college degree and then begin my career as a professional bass fisherman. I was accepted at Oregon State University, my school of choice. OSU drew my attention because of their Fisheries program. I figured if I had to go to college I might as well enjoy what I was going to study.

So in the summer of 1983, my last summer before starting college, I moved from Santa Barbara to my family's vacation home in Lincoln City, Oregon. I spent the summer there, fishing and working (mostly working). However, I had a great job with a landscaper—another opportunity to be outside every day along the Oregon coast.

By the summer of 1986, I had created enough of a reputation as a salmon fisherman to spend the whole summer working as a salmon guide on the Siletz River. I worked for myself and guided out of Coyote Rock Resort in the summer and fall for the tourists traveling up and down the Oregon Coast who wanted to go salmon fishing.

The Oregon coast is a fisherman's paradise. With the ocean, the rivers, and the natural lakes, there is no end to fishing opportunities. There was always a good bite going on somewhere, whether it was bass, salmon, or steelhead. When I was a kid, I can still recall getting lost in the assortment of angling opportunities on the coast. Each new day had an electric atmosphere, and I tingled with anticipation. I raced from one hot bite to the next, never quite satisfying my appetite for catching fish. I felt so full of life! I still feel more alive on the Oregon coast than any place on earth.

I had one small problem that summer. I spent most of the

summer without a boat. My dad had sold our boat in Santa Barbara because he didn't want me heading off to college with a boat as a distraction. He was a very wise man! He knew I would fish my way through five and six years of college or more if I had my boat. Towards the end of that first summer, I was desperate to go bass fishing. I needed a boat, and anything would do.

One day, while working on a landscaping job, I noticed an old dinghy in a woman's yard that she had been using as a creative flowerbed. However, she had recently decided to discard the old dinghy, and it was sitting over near a pile of junk. I couldn't believe it! A boat! A free boat at that! Containing my excitement, I asked her if I could please have her rotten dinghy. She eyeballed the junk pile as if to say, "What would he want with that old thing?" Nevertheless, she agreed to give it to me. So I had a buddy load it in the back of his truck and carry it down to Devils Lake—a 600-acre natural lake just 2 miles from my house in Lincoln City, Oregon.

I ASKED HER IF I COULD PLEASE HAVE HER ROTTEN DINGHY. SHE EYEBALLED THE JUNK PILE AS IF TO SAY, "WHAT WOULD HE WANT WITH THAT OLD THING?"

Devils Lake is right on the coast, boasting the distinction of having the world's shortest river flowing out of it. The "D" River flows all of about 150 yards from the Devils Lake to the Pacific Ocean. I had been fishing Devils Lake a little off the bank that summer and had caught a few bass from shore. Yet I was itching to get out there in a boat. An old timer who lived on the lake, Gary Fordyce, had taken me out fly-fishing a few times that summer in his little pram, and I knew the lake held bass.

No sooner did I have that dinghy down to the water than I had loaded it up with a battery and trolling motor, rod, reel, and tackle box. I pushed off shore and went bassin'. It may have cost me some funny looks from time to time, but I found a way to chase my dream! I must have been quite a sight—grinning from ear to ear—the proud owner of an old dinghy with a rotted out end. In fact, the whole transom was missing. I had to put all my

Focus

BY THE END OF THE SUMMER I SAVED ENOUGH MONEY TO BUY MY FIRST CAR. IF I HAD BEEN ANYWHERE ELSE IN THE COUNTRY, I AM SURE I WOULD HAVE BEEN TOO EMBARRASSED TO DRIVE SUCH A BEATER!

weight in the bow to keep the boat from filling with water! But, I sure caught 'em in that little rotten craft. I recall some delightful buzzbait action those summer evenings.

I didn't even have a place to keep that old rotten boat, but it turned out I didn't need one. At the end of the day, I would just pull it up and hide it in some brush on an undeveloped lot. I didn't care if anybody took it, and I didn't think anybody would. I was the only person in town for whom it held any value.

By the end of the summer I saved enough money to buy my first car. I had $1,500 to spend, and I settled on a five-year-old, rust colored (with real rust) Volkswagen® Rabbit. If I had been anywhere else in the country, I am sure I would have been too embarrassed to drive such a beater! I would have bought a truck or something much more macho. Thankfully, things are different up in Oregon where "earthy" is the going style.

On to Oregon State

By September, I was off to Corvallis, Oregon, for the beginning of my freshman year at Oregon State University (OSU). My old friend Brad was my college roommate. My mom and dad offered me a deal, and it was all I thought about that first year. They said if I got a respectable grade point average (G.P.A) my freshman year at OSU (at least a 3.0 out of 4.0), I could buy a boat that next summer. I must say that was a miserable first year, not having a boat. I had my car, so I drove to local lakes and caught a few bass from shore. I was new to the Wilamette Valley, and I didn't know any good bass ponds, so most of my fishing time that freshman year was on the North Fork of the Alsea River, the most popular nearby fishing spot, about a 45-minute drive from school. I caught my first steelhead trout that fall on November 15, which is very early for steelhead. It wasn't a giant, but I still remember taking it back to my dorm and cooking it (even though the pungent smell permeated the whole dorm)! Brad never missed another steelhead trip to the Alsea River after that day!

My G.P.A. hit a record level at the end of my freshman year at OSU—a lovely 3.6. I had the green light to work all summer to buy my first boat. I spent most of that summer working at the Chevron gas station at Salishan, a resort on the Oregon Coast just south of Lincoln City. I did some landscaping work for Loren Wands Landscaping and took up odd painting jobs as well, and by August I was the proud new owner of a 1968 14-foot Smokercraft, powered by a 1968 9.9 horsepower outboard. Painted yellow, it came on an old, rusted trailer—coordinating perfectly with my old, rusted Volkswagen.

Work Ethic

I NOW HAD A CAR AND A BOAT, AND I WAS ENTERING THE FAST LANE POWERED BY MY DREAM.

Life was good back then. On my days off from work, I fished the Siletz River in the morning for salmon then went to Devils Lake in the afternoon and caught bass. The bass in Devils Lake had never seen a buzzbait before. I had some of the best topwater fishing of my life back in those days. In a typical evening, I caught between ten and twenty bass on a buzzbait, up to six pounds. The lake had several boat docks, too, so I became a good dock fisherman as well.

I now had a car and a boat, and I was entering the fast lane powered by my dream. In the summer of 1984, Devils Lake was the perfect place for an aspiring young bass pro. Back then, Devils Lake had a weed problem. By August every summer, Eurasian Water Milfoil choked about a third of the lake. The pleasure boaters hated the stuff. But the bass loved it. I had a 600-acre lake loaded with grass and bass. I could fish out there all summer and never see another bass boat.

I caught my first steelhead while at Oregon State on the North Fork of the Alsea River, about a 45-minute drive from school. My college roommate, Brad, had slept in this morning, so I brought this fish back and threw it on his bed to wake him up! He never missed another steelhead trip to the Alsea after that day.

Learning to Win

For my sophomore year of college I headed back to Corvallis with my boat in tow. That year I found an apartment to rent, and it was a big relief to get out of the chaos of dorm life. I joined the Tenmile bass club that fall and fished a couple of club tournaments down on the coast. The first club tournament I ever fished was on Siltcoos Lake, and I won it. I didn't have much, not more than two bass at 8 pounds. I didn't do as well in the next club tournament on Tenmile Lake, but then I won the next club tournament in January on Lost Lake near Roseberg, Oregon.

That winter I got the itch to start fishing the big team tournaments in Oregon. The U.S. Bass Tournament Trail was the big deal back then. However, my boat was not tournament material. It would do for club tournaments, but it wasn't fit for big statewide team tournaments. I immediately began looking for a partner to fish with who had a boat. I remember picking up the phone and cold-calling Dave Wilson who ran the U.S. Bass Oregon Team circuit. I introduced myself, said I was a sophomore at OSU, and I wanted to fish his tournaments next spring. I asked him if he knew anyone with a bass boat who was looking for a partner. He promised to ask around and get back to me.

THAT WINTER I GOT THE ITCH TO START FISHING THE BIG TEAM TOURNAMENTS IN OREGON. I IMMEDIATELY BEGAN LOOKING FOR A PARTNER.

About a week later, a fellow named Steve Kastanes called me looking for a partner. Apparently, a friend of Steve's had received a call from the tournament director but didn't want to fish with "some college kid" who didn't know anything about tournament fishing, so this friend passed along my name to Steve. We started fishing together right away, and we became great friends and a great team.

I prefished all the tournaments in my little boat, and then fished the actual event in Steve's bass boat. In 1985, my first year of team tournament fishing, Steve and I finished fifth overall in the Oregon division of U.S. Bass that year and had numerous top-five finishes sprinkled throughout the year. It was a good first year of tournament fishing, all on new lakes for me. Steve was the perfect partner. Even though it was his boat, he always let me pick the water we fished, and I ran the trolling motor. That was a great situation for me to grow, learn, and improve as a bass fisherman.

The summer after my sophomore year of college, I really started to figure out how to catch those salmon in the Siletz

River and earn extra money as well. I worked for a landscaper in Lincoln City that summer, but because I had picked up salmon fishing so quickly, I also started doing a little guiding for salmon on the river. I could make as much money in a morning of salmon fishing as I could make in a whole day of landscaping! Of course, I liked guiding just a little bit better.

I WAS HUNGRY AND READY FOR MORE. WHILE STEVE WAS A GREAT FRIEND AND A WONDERFUL PERSON, WE HAD REACHED THE LIMIT OF HOW MUCH HE COULD TEACH ME.

I was hungry and ready for more. I told Steve I needed to change partners the following year. While Steve was a great friend and a wonderful person, we had reached the limit of how much he could teach me. I had the opportunity to fish with one of the top anglers in Oregon. In 1986, I teamed up with someone I knew from the tournaments, Jerry Harris—a longtime fisherman in Oregon and an experienced tournament winner who taught me a lot. We won four or five tournaments and capped off the season by winning the points race in the Oregon division of U.S. Bass. There were some tough teams with some talented fishermen in those days. Dub LaShot and Renaud Pelletier were a tough team, as were John Svec and Dave Pearson, Larry Slaughter and Harry Plouse, and Jeff Barnes and Dan Van Slyke.

Focus

In the spring, I arranged my classes at college so I went to school Tuesday, Wednesday, and Thursday, and fished the rest of the week. It was about a two and a half hour drive from Corvallis over to the coastal lakes. However, it seemed like nothing at all as I traveled in the wee hours of the morning to reach the coast. I remember many mornings setting my alarm for 2:30 a.m. and driving over to the coast, gear in tow, so I could be on the water by daylight. I wouldn't let any obstacles stand in the way of my fervent focus on fishing.

By the summer of 1986, I had created enough of a reputation as a salmon fisherman to spend the whole summer working as a salmon guide on the Siletz River. I worked for myself out of Coyote Rock Resort and guided tourists who wanted to go fishing. I had

A couple of nice jack salmon (small, immature males).

my best catch ever that summer and helped my clients catch four times the average number of those giant salmon. I recall we caught over eighty-seven that summer, including that year's bonus run of jack salmon (small immature males).

After having so much success at the local level, I was already beginning to formulate my post-graduation plans for the coming year. My goal to turn pro the next summer right after graduating college was beginning to take shape. I committed to graduate from OSU in four years, which is fairly unusual. Most kids take longer to get their degree, but I wanted out of there so I could begin my pro fishing career.

I switched my major after my freshman year to Resource Recreation Management, in the School of Forestry. My mind was always on fishing, though, not on the college classes. I learned how to do just enough work to pass my classes, so I could put most of my mental and physical energy into my fishing career. I remember all my peers thinking how odd it was for me to want to be a pro bass fisherman when I graduated. I didn't care one bit. I was driven, I was focused, and I didn't listen to what was popular or "in vogue" at the time. No wonder I didn't have too many friends in college!

Brad was still my best friend, but we began to drift apart as he pursued his chosen career in law enforcement. Not surprisingly, professional bass fishing didn't exactly make the "Top Ten" list of potentially lucrative career choices for college kids at that time. Especially in Oregon.

A few other students enjoyed salmon and steelhead fishing. In fact, a few professors enjoyed it as well. Not every student can say he skipped class with his professor to go fishing together! One of my professors had his own drift boat, and it wasn't unusual for us to skip class to go steelhead fishing now and then when the steelhead were really running in the Alsea River. I remember one time we skipped two days in a row. They were biting so good one day that we decided to head up there again the next day. I don't remember the professor's name, but I do remember the fish we caught!

I REMEMBER ALL MY PEERS THINKING HOW ODD IT WAS FOR ME TO WANT TO BE A PRO BASS FISHERMAN WHEN I GRADUATED. I DIDN'T CARE ONE BIT.

When my senior year at OSU rolled around in the spring of 1987, I knew I wouldn't finish out the tournament season because I planned to leave the state after graduation. Jerry wanted to fish the whole season with the same partner, but Steve Kastanes didn't mind if I teamed with him until I had to go. Steve and I did well in a couple of events that spring, and we won a big tournament that summer at Prineville Reservoir in central Oregon. I also made a trip to Lake Powell for the B.A.S.S. Western Federation Divisional. Back then, each team out West sent an eight-man team to the Divisional. The top man on the winning team qualified for the BASSMASTERS Classic. The Oregon team I was on included Dub La Shot, Renaud Pelletier, Clay Hood, Dan Jordon, Jeff Barnes, and others. We placed a close second to the Arizona team.

I left Oregon in June right after graduating from OSU to head south and begin fishing some national tournaments. My graduation present from Mom and Dad was a full size, late model Chevy cargo van. Nothing fancy, it was a good starter vehicle for a young man about to hit the tournament trail. My Volkswagen Rabbit had miraculously made it all the way through college. By the time I got rid of it that summer, it was about to disintegrate. It had a rusted out hole in the floorboard the size of a dinner plate!

My mom and dad loaned me the money that summer to buy my first bass boat. It was an 18-foot model, brand new. I didn't have sponsors at that point; we just went out and bought it from a dealer. There I was—a twenty-one-year-old kid fresh out of college with a new boat, a van, and a couple thousand dollars to my name. I felt ready to take on the world.

Family

I still get goose bumps every time I come here!

—My lifelong fishing mentor, Bill Sedar,
at eighty-eight years of age on a recent fishing trip
to Lake Cachuma.

Chapter Three

LEARNING FROM THE BEST

In 1982, few people in the world knew more about bass than Bill Sedar. Not only did Bill possess boundless wisdom on bass and how to catch them, but he also loved the challenge and had an unsurpassed passion for the sport. He was driven to catch them just like today's brightest fishing stars.

When I met Bill, the owner of Hook, Line and Sinker in Santa Barbara, I was a junior in high school. Bill was sixty-eight years old and I was sixteen years old—over fifty-one years of experience spanned between him and me. I was just beginning to pick up the game and wandered into his store one day with my friend, Brad, trying to pick out our first bass lures. I was full of desire and enthusiasm, but I knew nothing about the sport.

Bill had retired early at forty-six years of age to live his dream of bass fishing every day. He had fished Lake Cachuma an average of five days a week during those years. Think of the experience and wisdom he possessed after fishing the same 3,250-acre lake that frequently for the last twenty-two years. Put a winner like Bill on the same small lake five days a week for twenty-two years and you create a bass-catching machine of unprecedented proportions. He must have experienced every possible fishing condition—ten times! He knew every rock and twig in the lake. He had an intimate knowledge of those bass in

Bill Sedar at his favorite fishing spot, Lake Cachuma, near Santa Barbara, California.

Lake Cachuma. There have been very few men over the years that have understood bass the way Bill did. He knew all their habits, their likes, and dislikes. The lives of bass were totally exposed to Bill Sedar.

Mentoring

Bill laid the foundation for my fishing career, teaching me everything I know about bass. But the most important things Bill taught me were about the habits of the bass. That was his greatest strength. He knew everything about them. Bill knew what the bass did throughout the year and why they did it. The best part for me was learning through experience how he was dead-on with his teachings. He knew the truth about bass.

This information was invaluable to me. As a young, impressionable teenager just getting started in the sport of bass fishing, I was very susceptible to bad information. A lot of false information was floating around about bass fishing then (and still is today). Give a guy a $30,000 boat and enter him in a few bass tournaments, and he thinks he knows it all. I know God put Bill Sedar in my life, and I latched onto him like a tick to a hound dog.

Bill made his money inventing irrigation systems and by mastering the financial markets. He was a huge success at anything he put his hand to—and it didn't matter if it was business, fishing, golf, pool, or poker! Bill Sedar was a winner—an intense competitor who hated to lose. I've played a few games of pool and poker with him over the years, and I have never won. Not once! You'd think the old guy would feel sorry for me and just let me win occasionally. No way. Bill has been bass fishing for over fifty years, but he has never once fished a tournament. In fact, he is not widely known in bass fishing circles outside of Southern California. I would loved to have seen what Bill could have done in professional bass fishing. He would have accomplished much more in the sport than I have. Unfortunately, pro bass fishing came along too late for him.

Bill was a very versatile angler. Lake Cachuma, though it is small, has just about every kind of structure you can imagine. It has the main Santa Ynez River that feeds it, as well as five other smaller creeks. The lake has huge main lake flats that drop off into the main river channel, with smaller channels or drains running through them. Cachuma has seven islands, only one of which is above water at full pool. It has brush both shallow and deep including a few large trees, large weed beds in the summer and fall, roadbeds, walls, submerged bridges and cisterns, cement slabs, various sizes of river rock, shale rock, boulders, gravel, and sand. The water is mostly clear, but it can get very dingy after a good rain. The upper end was shallow, but at the dam it was 185 feet deep. I have never known a lake as small as Cachuma that had so many different types of structures and cover to fish. The lake even offers two types of bass: largemouth and smallmouth. Needless to say, a lot was there to keep Bill busy for over two decades. There were many ways to catch bass on the lake, and Bill learned them all. I couldn't have had a better lake to learn how to bass fish on than Cachuma.

THERE WERE MANY WAYS TO CATCH BASS ON THE LAKE, AND BILL LEARNED THEM ALL. I COULDN'T HAVE HAD A BETTER LAKE TO LEARN HOW TO BASS FISH ON THAN CACHUMA.

Bill taught me to use the whole lake and the whole tackle

box when bass fishing because that was how he fished. This is why I am so versatile. It was how I learned to fish from day one. Bill always told me if I wanted to catch bass every day, I had to be able to catch small ones as well as big ones. This meant becoming good with the plastic worm. Bill liked to fish the worm on a 6- or 8-pound line, so I learned finesse fishing. However, Bill's heart was not with the small ones you catch when worm fishing. His heart was with catching big bass—we called it his obsession.

Bill discovered that big bass have different life habits than small bass. There is a distinct difference between the two. Bill spent most of his later years exclusively chasing big bass, always with artificial lures. Bill is very efficient with all lures, but he is especially good with the 7-inch, 18S Rapala®, the 4-inch Rattlin' Rogue®, topwaters, and jigs. Those were his big fish baits. The hatchery trout stocked in Cachuma are a favorite staple of the big bass in the lake and a big draw, hence Bill's expertise with the "big Rappy," as he so fondly called it! That big 7-inch Rapala is one of the best trout imitation lures ever.

It might surprise some to learn for the last forty-two years

My mentor, Bill Sedar, is not only fervent about his fishing; he is still wildly in love with his beautiful bride, Barbara. After more than fifty years of marriage, he still has a sparkle in his eye for the love of his life.

Bill has fished out of nothing but a 14-foot aluminum rental boat. It is all he needs. He's that good. Bill has used a trolling motor and a portable flasher over the years, but that is the extent of his on-board technology. Bill says he prefers the smaller boat in Cachuma's clear waters because it casts a smaller shadow. He is pretty good with the oars as well, but that is one skill I never picked up!

BILL LOVES LIFE, AND HE LIVES EACH DAY WITH A CONTAGIOUS PASSION. AS HE IDLES OUT OF CACHUMA HARBOR FOR A MORNING OF FISHING, HE IS SO EXCITED THAT HE FREQUENTELY BREAKS OUT IN SONG AT THE TOP OF HIS LUNGS!

Besides all the bass catching expertise Bill gave me, the other invaluable quality he possessed was a genuine, childlike enthusiasm for each day on the water. His passion and zeal for the people and the activities he loved are perhaps his greatest legacy. Bill loves life, and he lives each day with a contagious passion. As he idles out of Cachuma harbor for a morning of fishing, he is so excited that he frequently breaks out in song at the top of his lungs! On my most recent fishing trip with Bill, in November of 2002, as we turned off the highway and drove past the ranger station on our way to Cachuma Marina, he quipped with glee, "I still get goose bumps every time I come here!" He was eighty-eight years old when he made that remark, and it was probably his 10,000th day of fishing on the same lake. What unbelievable fire this man has for life!

The common thread from my high school days through my college years, and throughout my pro career, is my relationship with Bill Sedar. Over the last twenty-two years, no one has taught me more about fishing. Bill knows the sport, but he is also a gifted teacher. Playing a sport well and teaching it effectively don't often go hand in hand. To know Bill and to have such an awesome fisherman and teacher in my life is such a blessing.

Mentoring

Outside of the first two years of our initial meeting when I was a high school student, the rest of our relationship has been long distance, but accountability has kept it going. Bill and I have kept in touch at least once a month by letter or phone for over twenty years. Sometimes we'll even be in contact twice in a month. That steady communication is our accountability. He reinforces the basics to me and asks me questions when I'm going through a dry spell in my fishing, checking me to see where the problem is. I have made a special trip back to Lake Cachuma to fish with Bill every year for the last fourteen years.

Way Beyond Fishing

Mentoring is one of the most effective ways to influence another person. Mentoring relationships have played an integral role in my success over the years. In fact, these relationships have played such a powerful role I can't imagine how I would or even could be where I am today without the special mentors in my life. Bill Sedar was the perfect mentor for me, and some might agree it was a match "made in heaven." I happen to be fifty-one years younger than Bill, yet he sees so much of himself in me. Likewise, I see in him the man I would like to become. God gave me a mentor who taught me, and he gave Bill a special mentoring relationship he had never had with a young man. It goes way past fishing—we're like family.

I CAN'T IMAGINE HOW I WOULD OR EVEN COULD BE WHERE I AM TODAY WITHOUT THE SPECIAL MENTORS IN MY LIFE.

A mentor makes you accountable in many areas of life. It is so important for young people to have elders as good role models who are willing to take the time to pass on their wisdom and experience. These men and women lead by example. Older women can teach younger women and mature men can advise young men on how to live their lives in a positive way. I believe anyone younger than thirty years of age can use a mentor as a guide. I had an advantage on all the other sixteen-year-old

Here I am joining Bill Sedar, and my best friend and college roommate, Brad Sharpton, in 1989 on Lake Cachuma. I had been a pro about two years at this time.

aspiring bass pros in the country. Throughout my high school years, and then for the next twenty years, Bill has been there for me every step of the way.

I'm afraid there are not as many mentors as there used to be. In America, we are becoming a self-centered nation that is primarily concerned with taking care of self. We are busy people, running faster than ever just to make ends meet. I know from experience that at the end of the day, there is little time left to mentor a young person. However, if we don't make time for the things that are important for the future of our community, country, and world, then mentoring will become a lost art in America.

We are not born knowing how to live. We learn best by example. Unfortunately, many parents neglect their influential role. Consequently, kids look to each other for coaching to fill in the gap. And that's not always a pretty sight. Kids today are desperately searching for clues on what it means to be a young man or woman. I am so thankful for the men in my life who have taken the time to share life-lessons with me and contribute to my generation.

Learning to Mentor

The mentoring process has somehow gained an undesirable reputation over the years. Many older adults shy away from mentoring because they think of it as a formal institution and figure they don't have the training or expertise to mentor someone. Nothing could be farther from the truth. Most of what happens in mentoring is "caught," not taught. It's not like a teacher-student situation where a teacher hands out information on a page. Mentoring simply means coming alongside someone in the context of a relationship to show him or her how to live. Maybe you know a young adult dealing with some of the same challenges and obstacles you once faced. What do you wish someone had told you then that you know now? That's the role of a mentor.

MOST OF WHAT HAPPENS IN MENTORING IS "CAUGHT," NOT "TAUGHT." IT'S NOT LIKE A TEACHER-STUDENT SITUATION WHERE A TEACHER HANDS OUT INFORMATION ON A PAGE.

The desire to mentor starts with a desire to make the world a better place. Family often proves to be a good starting point. An adult may know a younger niece or nephew needing direction. The sense of obligation we feel toward family can be very motivating. From what I've learned in my own experience, the mentor relationship, as in any relationship, must be a two-way street in terms of communication and commitment.

A mentor must be unselfish, giving, caring, and have a desire to commit a big part of his or her life into a younger person.

Not every young person is ready to be mentored. The student must recognize the fact that he or she doesn't already know everything. The student must be teachable, a good listener and willing to pick up coaching tips from everyday life experiences. Most importantly, the student must have a burning desire to learn and succeed.

If you decide to be a mentor for someone, be great friends with that person. What do you have in common? The same career interests? The same type of family? Mentors spend time with their students, developing trust in order to earn the right to be heard. Eat dinner together once a month. Go to a ball game. The relationships I have with the mentors in my life are pure bliss. Why? Because we are the best of friends.

Although a relationship is key, spending time with a friend is different from spending time with a mentor. In fact, I believe there are three levels of relationships we all must have. We all have peers—friends who are on the same level with us. They are typically the same age and think similarly to us emotionally, relationally and spiritually.

MENTORS ARE USUALLY OLDER THAN US AND THEY HAVE SOMETHING WE DON'T HAVE, NAMELY WISDOM, KNOWLEDGE, SKILLS, AND STRATEGIES THAT COME FROM HAVING EXPERIENCED MORE OF LIFE.

However, mentors are usually older than us and they have something we don't have, namely wisdom, knowledge, skills, and strategies that come from having experienced more of life. Finally, as potential mentors we need a student—someone who is younger and knows less than we do and can benefit from our wisdom and experience.

Young people have to be careful about their choice of mentor. One of the pitfalls of a poor choice is to wind up with someone who is not good at his or her craft. Misguided mentors who mistakenly think they know what they're talking about can mess up a young life in a hurry. A mentor should have a proven record of accomplishment as a winner for many years. A mentor who talks like a winner must also have the proof of being successful in a particular craft or business to back it up. A misguided mentor can mess up your heart and your outlook on life. Make sure your mentor is a quality individual. Is that person a man or woman of integrity? What do friends and colleagues say about his or her character? Where are they spiritually? Be careful to choose wisely.

"Can a blind man lead a blind man? Will they not both fall into a pit? A student is not above his teacher, but everyone who is fully trained will be like his teacher," (Luke 6:39–40).

Lasting Legacy

Lately, Bill Sedar the husband has had more of an impact on me than Bill Sedar the fisherman. Bill is still wildly in love with his beautiful bride, Barbara. After more than fifty years of marriage, he still has a sparkle in his eye for his wife. Bill and Barbara set the standard for my wife Jill and me when it comes to romance. Their love is as pure and beautiful as any I have ever seen.

Mentoring

BILL'S LEGACY WILL BE THE HIGH STANDARD HE HAS SET FOR A GENERATION, AND THAT'S QUITE A GIFT.

Bill McCartney, the president of the national men's group Promise Keepers, has said that you can tell the worth of a man by observing the countenance of his wife. A woman whose husband fully loves her definitely stands out because she is full of joy. She is fulfilled; her life is complete. She is secure and has great confidence in her man. Bill Sedar's wife Barbara seems to glow with a love for Bill that radiates from her eyes and her smile. Barbara has suffered from a severe case of Alzheimer's these past few years. At eighty-eight years of age, he still lovingly and tenderly meets all her needs on a daily basis. He sacrifices his desires to meet her needs. She now requires twenty-four-hour care, and he is right there for her. Bill's legacy will be the high standard he has set for my generation, and that's quite a gift.

I hope I can one day be half the man that Bill Sedar is. I just thank God he put that man in my life. Bill loves God, he is an awesome husband, and he has been a good father to his four children. He is a winner at everything he touches. He was so successful at business, he was able to retire at forty-six. He was so successful as a fishing mentor that his star student became a World Champion.

SECTION TWO:
DESIRE

Don't rush your dreams.
Desire must be tempered with wisdom and patience.

—My advice to young people
who have their hearts set on a dream.

Chapter Four

THE EARLY YEARS AS A PRO

I was at a good place in my life in the summer of 1987. For four years I had worked toward getting my college degree—something my mom, dad, and anyone with good common sense agreed I should do—plus I had been successful in state-level bass tournaments. Those college years gave me a chance to mature both as a person and as a fisherman. While in school, my desire to enter the pro bass fishing world percolated, and I was so ready by the time I graduated that nothing could hold me back from charging headlong into my dream. Lacking a college degree certainly would not have stopped me, but I tell kids all the time not to rush their dreams. Desire must be tempered with wisdom and patience.

In contrast, I have seen aspiring bass fishermen loaded with talent burst into the national tournament scene too early. When young pros don't temper their ambition, they often meet with disaster. One of the biggest reasons not to rush your dreams is that the fishing industry is relatively small and you only get one chance at the endorsement game. One bad mistake that tarnishes your reputation can mean your endorsement opportunities are over. Don't let your desire outpace your ability to handle all that comes with reaching your dreams.

Patience

Go West, Young Man

I had never felt so full of joy as when I headed south out of Oregon on I-5 towards Lake Mead near Las Vegas, Nevada, after graduation. I headed to Mead by myself to prepare for my first pro tournament, the U.S. Open. Excitement surged through every fiber of my being. I was finally free! There was no place in the world I would rather have been than on that road—in that van. I arrived at Lake Mead within a couple of days. I knew nothing about the place except what I had read in *U.S. Bass* and *West Coast Bass* magazines. I didn't even know where to stay, so I just pulled into Callville Bay and set up camp by myself.

In mid-June near Las Vegas, the highs each day were at least 110 degrees, and the lows at night were around 85 degrees on a cool night. I learned some lessons the hard way right away. I had never before fished in that kind of heat. In fact, I had spent the first part of that summer fishing on the Oregon Coast where the daily highs were in the 60s most days. All I packed in the boat to

Weighing in at my first pro BASSMASTER on Lake Mead in April of 1989. I caught the largest fish of the tournament and the largest stringer.

drink on my first day out on Lake Mead were two 12-ounce cans of Pepsi. Later that day, I came into Callville Bay Marina around 3:00 p.m. to watch a local tournament weigh-in, and I was feeling a little sick to my stomach. I was getting worse by the second; I never even made it to the weigh-in! Instead, I went to lie down in my van. I lay there in the searing heat for about an hour, feeling like I was about to die! I finally figured out I was dehydrated. Man, I had a lot to learn!

I prefished Mead for two weeks, and then it went "off-limits" for the tournament participants, as the rules require. During the off-limits, I drove down to Scottsdale, Arizona, to stay with my Uncle Bill and Aunt Mary Ann. My Aunt Shirley and my grandmother had also moved there from New York, so we had a bit of a reunion. They were nice enough to let me stay at their place until the tournament started. My dad flew into Phoenix before the tournament and drove up to Mead with me to show his support. He spent the week with me at a hotel in Las Vegas.

To say I was pumped to fish the U.S. Open is a bit of an understatement. I recall waking up at 2:45 a.m. each day during that tournament. I'd eat breakfast in the casino then make the hour-long drive to the lake, arriving early for the 5:30 a.m. take-off. I have always been an early bird my whole career. I don't like being in a hurry that early in the morning, so I sacrificed a little sleep to beat the rush at the boat ramp. I had a great tournament. I was in fifth place after the first day, and I remember having to get up in front of everybody that night at the press conference to tell about my day. It was my first day to ever fish in a national tournament, and I was in fifth place! All the big-name pros were there: Rick Clunn, Larry Nixon, Roland Martin, Gary Klien, Denny Brauer and Jimmy Houston. You name it; they were all there—all my heroes I had been reading about during my four years in college.

TO SAY I WAS PUMPED TO FISH THE U.S. OPEN IS A BIT OF AN UNDERSTATEMENT. I RECALL WAKING UP AT 2:45 A.M. EACH DAY... ARRIVING EARLY FOR THE 5:30 A.M. TAKE-OFF.

I finished fifth at the Red Man Regional at Ute Lake, New Mexico in November of 1989. These two bass qualified me to go on to my first Red Man All American in Buffalo, New York.

I ended up taking sixth place at the end of the four-day tournament. I caught most of my fish ripping a spinnerbait in the Virgin River. I won $8,000 that week, which bankrolled me for the rest of the summer. Larry Hopper of California won that U.S. Open with 23 pounds total after four days of fishing! That was the toughest U.S. Open to date. I had caught about 19 pounds. I like to think that if I had known then what I know now things would have been different! But, in this sport, it doesn't always work that way.

With my first pro tournament such a big success, I was ready for more. I had the green light from my aunt and uncle in Scottsdale to stop by their place and stay anytime I wished, but

I spent most of my time on the road, fishing small tournaments in Arizona that fall. Desert fishing was all new to me. I don't recall having much success that fall. The fish were all deep, and I was a shallow water guy. Since I couldn't catch them shallow, I'd move out deep but I couldn't catch them there either!

John Murray was the local fishing ace of Roosevelt Lake, the largest lake in the Arizona desert, some 80 miles northeast of Phoenix. John was winning every tournament in sight that fall—something like nine tournaments in a row. He was the only guy who had figured out those deep, suspended fish. To this day, I don't know how he caught them. His is still the most dominating performance I have ever seen by one fisherman on one lake. David Fritts could also totally dominate fishing during a certain season of the year. The fish suspend away from cover in the fall, and these two guys have found unparalleled success at catching them.

John's outstanding performance that fall was a great inspiration to me. Not only was he winning everything, but he and I were the same age, about twenty-two years old. My plans called for me to be the top fisherman in that neck of the woods, and John was standing in my way! I had a lot to learn because he was whipping me at the tournaments like a schoolboy.

An Olympic Sport

When Thanksgiving rolled around, the tournaments ended for the year. I parked my boat at my Uncle Bill's house and flew to see my family for the holidays. Mom and Dad were back in Honolulu, so the idea of heading to the islands for a month sounded great to me. Unfortunately I wasn't able to live like the average twenty-one-year-old on vacation in Hawaii. Instead of heading to the beach and the party scene, I went to work. I had thousands of dollars in tournament entry fees coming up that next spring and no money. The only way I was going to be able to fish was to make some cash.

I really worked hard that Christmas—working three jobs a week. I sold fresh seafood at a store during the day. Then I went down to Waikiki each evening to serve up ice cream cones at the local Haagen-Dazs® store. On weekends, I helped my dad paint a

Work
Ethic

friend's house. I don't think I went to the beach one time during that month in Hawaii. I was focused, baby! Even as I slapped Mint Chocolate Chip into cups and cones, I was thinking about John Murray and all those western boys. I had them in my sights, and I was determined I was going to beat them that next year.

AT THAT TIME, I FELT THE ONLY THING KEEPING ME FROM REALIZING MY DREAM OF BECOMING A TOP BASS PRO WAS MYSELF.

After that month in Hawaii, I started treating bass fishing as if it were an Olympic sport. I took an unrestrained approach to bass fishing. I trained for competition the way I envisioned an Olympic athlete trained for his sport. I was hungry and unbelievably focused. There were no wasted days.

At this time in my life, I had no distractions from building my career. After graduating from college, my social life didn't improve, but at least fishing no longer had to compete with finals. With no school, no girlfriend, no debt, and no commitments, I had absolute freedom to chase my dream.

Focus

At that time, I felt the only thing keeping me from realizing my dream of becoming a top bass pro was myself. Anglers have no one to blame in this solitary sport. We have no coaches, no teammates, no partners, and no boss. I liked it that way. I have always held to the adage that says, "If you want something done right, you have to do it yourself." During my "Olympic" training regime, I lived bass fishing twenty-four hours a day, seven days a week for the next year and a half. I fished from dawn to dusk, every day. If I was not on the water fishing, I was either driving to the next tournament or getting my engine fixed. That was my life. I sacrificed everything else to compete at the highest level possible. Life was so simple back then. Catching bass was my only care in the world.

In January 1988, after my working vacation, I came back from Hawaii and hit the western tournament trails. I had talked earlier in the year with my dad and my Uncle Bill about how many tournaments I should fish. Originally, I thought about picking

At the boat dock of my first Red Man All American in Buffalo, New York, 1990. The All American is an amateur championship for aspiring pros and weekend fishermen alike. For that reason, this minor league championship is often referred to as a "working man's" world championship. It was a perfect tournament for an aspiring pro like me, and I finished sixth.

just a few big tournaments and spending a lot of time preparing for them. However, my dad and uncle recommended that I fish as many tournaments as I could to gain as much experience as possible right away. They were right. I spent the next three years fishing everything I could get my hands on out West. I fished about forty tournaments each year. There were four or five tournament circuits out West back then, and I fished them all.

Hitting the Trail

Focus

The first Red Man® Tournament was in early February 1988, on Lake Havasu in Arizona. I spent the last week of January down there prefishing. The weather was nasty. I woke up some mornings to cold, wind, and heavy rain. However, I still went fishing—all day long. That was my job. There was no deciding whether to fish or not each day; I had made the decision not to waste a day a long time ago. I didn't give myself a choice—that's what discipline is all about. Most of the veteran guys would stay indoors on days like that. The few of them I had met, like Okie Vaughn, Buck Brown, and Lyall Grant, could tell I had the "eye of the tiger!"

I did not know a single person going into the partner pairings before that tournament. I was the new kid fresh out of Oregon, they were all new competitors, and the lakes were all new to me. I reminded myself, "Nobody here knows me--but they will!" Recognition didn't take long. I should have won that first Red Man; I could have blown it away, but I lost a few good fish. I finished second. However, I ended up winning Angler of the Year in the Red Man Colorado River Division that year. Then I went on to the Red Man Tournament of Champions in Honolulu, Hawaii, in December 1988 and won that, too. My career was taking off.

I WOKE UP SOME MORNINGS TO COLD, WIND, AND HEAVY RAIN. HOWEVER I STILL WENT FISHING ALL DAY LONG.

My success wasn't just on the Red Man Tournament Trail. In the next two years, I won tournaments on every lake on the Colorado River: Powell, Mead, Mohave, Havasu, and Martinez. I won on Roosevelt, San Carlos, and Elephant Butte. I won West Coast Bass tournaments, All Star Bass tournaments, Sun Country Bass tournaments, and a U.S. Bass pro draw tournament on Lake Mohave.

I got on such a roll in the fall and winter of 1988-89 that I won five tournaments in a row, all on different lakes. Western Outdoor News (WON) began their new WON BASS tournament trail in November 1988 on Lake Powell. I won that. The December win at the Red Man Tournament of Champions in Hawaii brought the total to two. The second stop on the WON BASS trail was a few weeks later in January at Lake Havasu. Another win. (I went on to win the WON BASS Angler of the Year title in 1989.) A couple weeks later, I went back to Havasu and won the first Red Man of the 1989 season, making it four tournament wins in a row.

At one point toward the end of my string of victories, I remember my old nemesis, John Murray, chiding me in a half-serious, half-joking tone, "I can't believe you have won four tournaments in a row." He continued, "But the next tournament is on Roosevelt, and that's my home lake. You won't do well there. If you win that one, too, I'll kill you," he joked. I knew just as he did that I had never won on Roosevelt. In fact, I had always struggled on Roosevelt. However, as it turned out, I won that tournament, too, and sent John Murray into orbit! This was an unbelievable winning streak! Every top fisherman in the West was in those tournaments, which made my five wins in a row all the sweeter.

Playing with the Big Boys

The Bass Anglers Sportsmans Society (B.A.S.S.), the major league of competitive bass fishing, brought their tournament trail to Lake Mead in April of 1989. It was one of their last stops on their 1988-89 circuit. They had a few openings in the field, and they accepted me for the event. I couldn't wait to make some strides fishing in a big league tournament. I had competed against the best western bass fishermen. However, the guys who fished B.A.S.S. were the best fishermen in the whole country. And they were coming to my lake where I was having so much success!

I was thrilled to finish twelfth in that first B.A.S.S. tournament–not bad for a young up and coming pro! I even caught the largest stringer and the biggest bass of the whole event on the final day while fishing with Mark Davis, a top pro from Arkansas.

I noticed right away that his skills were far superior to anyone I'd ever been paired with in a tournament. This was a new level of competition for me. I was especially impressed with the way Mark was able to find quality bass during his first trip to fish Lake Mead. When I caught the largest stringer and the largest bass, my friends out West were not surprised—I had already proven myself to them. I was really glad I had performed so well in my first pro tournament; it boosted my confidence and confirmed I was on the right track. Even so, I was still a no-name at this point amid all those seasoned pros.

My dedication, focus, and training were paying off at a rapid pace. Within two years of my college graduation, I moved up from a no-name kid to the top of the western tournament trails. I won at least one tournament on every lake on the Colorado River chain. Those lakes are still some of my favorite places to bass fish, especially Lake Powell. I was able to pay my parents back for the loan on my first boat, and I had saved about $80,000 in winnings.

EVERYTHING WAS ON TRACK, BUT MY LIFE WAS ABOUT TO GET MORE COMPLEX. MY DAYS OF FOCUSING SOLELY ON FISHING WOULD SOON END.

Everything was on track, but my life was about to get more complex. My days of focusing solely on fishing would soon end. I was beginning to pick up a few sponsors like Skeeter® Boats, Daiwa® rods and reels, and Berkley PowerBait. They had seen promise in my future, and they came calling. I began the process of learning to deal with sponsors, a key element in a bass fisherman's future. I knew it was impossible to make a living off tournament winnings; every successful bass fisherman has to have his share of endorsements in order to make it on the Tour.

Patience

At this point in my relationships with sponsors, I mainly used their products and promoted them among fisherman at fishing seminars or tackle shows. It was an entry level position where sponsors "pay for potential," hoping you'll become more successful. However, as you become more successful, your relationship with your sponsors increases proportionately. They want more of your time. At the top level of professional bass fishing, manufacturers often use their high profile pros as a major marketing tool through print advertisements, television, personal appearances, etc. However, at this point, I was just starting out in the endorsement game. I could already see how this new dynamic would take more time away from fishing.

After two years of intense competition, I sensed a change inside me. I got to the point where I needed a little social life. Today I refer to this as my "hormonal shift!" I finally admitted I couldn't continue with that kind of training intensity forever. I started wondering what I had been missing all those years socially. I'd had some good success at fishing, and I was ready to see what else life had to offer. That was when I met the love of my life, Miss Jill Montgomery.

A Gorgeous Smile

By January of 1989, I had worn out my welcome at my aunt and uncle's place in Arizona. For the last year and a half, I had used their house as a stopping off point between tournaments. I usually stayed a couple of days, did my laundry, and then headed off again. I finally realized I couldn't live like a vagrant forever. Plus, I had made enough money fishing to at least rent an apartment. However, Phoenix was a big city, and I didn't have a clue how to find the right apartment.

I thumbed through the phone book one day and found the address of an apartment locator agency. The representative said she had just the place for a fisherman like me—Bay Club Apartments. She said it wrapped around a lake loaded with fish. Perfect! When we arrived, Jill was the leasing agent who greeted me. Her beauty and gorgeous smile instantly captured me. It took me a couple of days to get up the nerve to ask her out, but to my relief she accepted! I took her out to a nice steakhouse, and we hit it off right away. The next day, not knowing anything better to do, I took her to the Phoenix Open golf tournament. We got along so well that day that I decided to try my luck and ask Jill out again.

I met the love of my life, Miss Jill Montgomery, in 1989 while living in Phoenix, Arizona.

On our next date, we went fishing on Bartlett Lake, just outside of Phoenix. When we got to the busy boat ramp, I told Jill to go ahead and jump in the boat. I wanted to launch the boat before looking for a parking space. I unhooked the bow, backed it down the ramp, and mashed the brakes. The boat slid off the trailer and out into the lake. No problem. I drove my van up the hill to find a parking spot. It took a while, and by the time I got back down to the ramp, the wind had pushed Jill out to sea! She looked pretty worried, floating way out there all by herself. I yelled to her from the pier, "Put the trolling motor down and come get me!" At that point, the girl of my dreams yelled back, "What's a trolling motor?"

As she drifted farther and farther away from me, I flinched and thought, "Oh, no. This isn't good. I just lost my girl and my boat!" I took a deep breath and came back with, "Then just start the big motor and idle over here!" She retorted, "How? I don't know how to start a boat!" By this time, we had attracted quite a bit of attention, with at least a dozen boats waiting to use the ramp. "Just turn the key!" I hollered back.

Finally, some gracious boaters helped pull her to the dock. Boy, was she ever upset! Relationships were all new to me, and I was learning on the fly how to handle a girlfriend. Jill was more than a little embarrassed in front of all those people. She didn't speak to me for at least an hour. I remember thinking, "That's the end of this romance." Fortunately, she gave me a second chance.

I YELLED TO HER FROM THE PIER, "PUT THE TROLLING MOTOR DOWN AND COME GET ME!" AT THAT POINT, THE GIRL OF MY DREAMS YELLED BACK, "WHAT'S A TROLLING MOTOR?"

Life was beginning to change and grow more complex for me. Adding a serious girlfriend as well as sponsors to my daily activities took time away from my fishing routine. Instead of blocking out whole days of fishing, I had to make sure I scheduled time to go to tackle shows and other fishing events to promote my sponsors' products. Not to mention, I was also busy scheduling dates with Jill!

Of course, I enjoyed being with Jill, and I appreciated the necessary financial benefits of having sponsors. These were positive additions to my lonely, self-centered existence. I welcomed the changes, even if they put a short-term drag on my tournament performance. I had to adjust to the limitations on my fishing time. In the long run, I wanted a wife like Jill, and I needed sponsors to make it as a pro, so I figured I had better get used to the changes. Dealing with change was a necessary part of maturing from a kid to a man.

Patience

Getting My Attention

Later that same year, another experience got my attention and changed my happy-go-lucky existence. One night in Phoenix, I dreamed my father, who was living back in Hawaii, had just been diagnosed with cancer. It was a powerful, vivid dream—I awoke with a sinking feeling in my heart that stayed with me all morning. I wasn't prone to having dreams, so it really got my attention. Later that day my mom called me while I was out on the golf course. "Son, the doctors just diagnosed Dad with cancer," she said. I couldn't believe what she was telling me. Not only did my dad have cancer, but I had just dreamed that very scenario.

That was my first experience with something I consider "otherworldly"–my first encounter with the spiritual realm. God was starting to get my attention. My father wasn't supposed to get sick. He was the picture of health, jogging forty miles per week. I thought, "If cancer could hit him, it could hit anybody, including me." For the first time in my life, my own mortality began to come into view.

Ready for the Major Leagues

Fishing the top western circuits was probably similar to a minor league baseball experience. I played every day, gained lots of experience, and had great success. You could say I was the Most Valuable Player at the AAA level. After three years with that kind of record, I felt like I was ready for the big leagues. In 1989, that meant the BASSMASTER Tournament Trail.

I signed up for the 1989/90 BASSMASTER Invitationals. Back then, there was only one division of Invitationals, and the events were spread out all over America. The first tournament was on the St. Lawrence River in upstate New York. It took me forty-five hours to tow my boat up there from Phoenix. Then I bombed in the tournament, and I had to relive each miserable moment in my mind during the forty-five hour drive home.

The second event on the schedule that season was at Lake

Havasu in Arizona—a lake I knew very well. I placed tenth in the tournament, but something even more significant happened during that tournament. On the first day, they paired me with a fellow named Terry Chupp. Terry was an evangelist and led the once-a-week Fellowship of Christian Anglers Society (FOCAS) meetings at each BASSMASTER tournament. FOCAS is a nondenominational gathering for fellowship, singing, and an informal time of prayer and Bible study. Terry and I had a good time together that day, even though he asked me some tough questions.

While we were fishing, Terry asked me about what he called my "spiritual heritage." I tossed out a quick answer about attending church with my parents quite a bit in my youth. Sensing he wasn't satisfied, I also offered a couple of heroic stories about my Grandpa's days as an overseas missionary. Even that wasn't enough for him. He asked me if I knew Jesus Christ and if I was "saved."

WHILE WE WERE FISHING, TERRY ASKED ME ABOUT WHAT HE CALLED MY "SPIRITUAL HERITAGE." I TRIED TO CHANGE THE SUBJECT.

I was not a Christian at the time, so I tried to change the subject when Terry asked about my personal relationship with the Lord. From that day forward, Terry faithfully invited me to attend one of the FOCAS meetings every time our paths crossed at a tournament. Not wanting to hurt his feelings but not wanting to commit either, I'd always give him some half-hearted hope that I might attend. But I never did.

Even though I turned Terry down for the next three and half years, Terry never lost his enthusiasm for inviting me. I did not attend a FOCAS meeting until three and a half years later at a tournament down in Georgia in February of 1993. Looking back now, I see God had been trying to get my attention for years, but I wasn't listening.

The next BASSMASTER tournament that first season was in January of 1990, at Lake Okeechobee in south Florida. That one took thirty-eight hours to drive one way. Fortunately, Jill agreed to come with me. She had been to a few local tournaments in Arizona with me, but this was her first road trip. Money was tight then, so we camped at Anglers Marine in Clewiston in my conversion van. She stepped in a huge pile of fire ants one night while trying to find the restroom. I bombed in the tournament. I thought she would never want to go to another tournament with me again! We drove home to Phoenix nursing her ant bites and my bruised ego. We agreed that if I was going to keep fishing the BASSMASTER Tour, we had to move closer to the action. We began talking seriously about moving East.

I WAS DISAPPOINTED I DIDN'T MAKE IT TO MY GOAL OF FISHING THE BASSMASTERS CLASSIC. I DISCOVERED IT WAS TOUGH TO COMPETE ON LAKES AND RIVERS THAT WERE NEW TO ME, AND I REALIZED I HAD A LOT TO LEARN.

I didn't make money in any other B.A.S.S. tournaments on the trail that season except for the April 1990 tournament at Lake Powell where I finished sixth. I was disappointed I didn't make it to my goal of fishing the BASSMASTERS Classic. I was very competitive on the water I knew well, posting tenth at Havasu and sixth at Powell. However, I had never seen the other stops on the Tour that year: the St Lawrence River, Lake Okeechobee, Sam Rayburn, and Lake Guntersville. I discovered it was tough to compete on lakes and rivers that were new to me, and I realized I had a lot to learn.

That first season on the Tour ended in May of 1990. In June, I fished in my first Red Man All American in Buffalo, New York. I had fished the Colorado River division of Red Man in 1988 and 1989, winning the points championship both years. I bombed in the 1988 Regional tournament but did well enough in the 1989 Regional to qualify for the All American that year on Lake Erie. The All American is an amateur championship for aspiring pros and weekend fishermen alike. For that reason, this minor league championship is often referred to as the "working man's" world championship. It was a perfect tournament for an aspiring pro like me. We had fun up there in Buffalo, and I finished sixth.

Taking the Leap

Jill and I headed back to Phoenix for the rest of the summer. That July, we traveled up to Lincoln City, Oregon, to visit some family and enjoy some cool weather. We had been dating for one and a half years, and it was time to make a commitment. I had a clever plan for popping the question.

I took Jill salmon fishing on the Siletz River. We anchored up in Windy Bend, my favorite haunt from days gone by. I had dug up some live sand shrimp for bait that day. I knew Jill didn't like to touch them, so I lovingly offered to bait her hook for her. We fished for about thirty minutes and all was quiet. It was time for a new shrimp on her hook, so she reeled in and gave me the end of her line.

I QUICKLY CUT OFF HER HOOK, TIED A DIAMOND RING ON THE END OF HER LINE, AND SLIPPED THE WHOLE RIG BACK IN THE RIVER BEFORE SHE COULD SEE. I WAS TENSE TO SAY THE LEAST.

With my back turned to her, I quickly cut off her hook, tied a diamond ring on the end of her line, and slipped the whole rig back in the river before she could see. We were fishing vertically, straight under the boat, in about 30 feet of water. Jill casually hit the free spool on her Daiwa reel and sent the ring down to the bottom. Even though I tied the ring to 30-pound Trilene® XT, I was tense to say the least. I had saved a long time for that rock! After the longest five minutes of my life, I calmly suggested, "Honey, why don't you reel in an check your bait?" What a surprise! We had a big party that night with some family and friends and set a wedding date for July 6, 1991.

Go East, Young Man

When our engagement began, we started making firm plans to move east later that summer. Eighty percent of the big fishing tournaments in the country are in the Southeast, so it made good sense to live there. We contemplated a few places, but we settled on moving to East Texas to be close to what I thought would be a good home lake–Sam Rayburn Lake. I knew nothing about grass fishing or fishing southern lowland lakes, so I thought Rayburn would provide a good training ground for me.

IN AUGUST OF 1990, WE LOADED UP MY VAN AND MY SKEETER BOAT WITH ALL OF OUR BELONGINGS AND MADE THE PIGRIMAGE EAST.

In August of 1990, we loaded up my van and my Skeeter boat with all of our belongings and made the pilgrimage east. Jill and I were West Coast natives, boldly heading off to a new frontier. In contrast to our ancestors, the mantra of an aspiring young bass pro in 1990 was "Go east young man, go east!"

We crammed everything we owned into that van and boat. We were afraid to stop for the night with all our gear in the boat, so we drove straight through from Phoenix to Sam Rayburn, about twenty-two hours. Jill and I were both twenty-four years old at the time, and everything seemed like a new adventure. We rented a condominium at a country resort called Rayburn Country when we first arrived in Texas, then we found a trailer to rent right on the shores of the lake in a little subdivision close to the dam.

Courage

Moving meant I was gambling everything on the unknown. However, I was still young. I had risen to the top of every level I had fished. Therefore, I believed I had the potential to do the same on a national level. That was not a foolish gamble; it was a calculated risk. Even so, I didn't consider it a risk. I was chasing my dream of being a top bass pro–doing what I loved to do.

From a business standpoint, I took on substantial risk to pursue growth. I gave up a sure thing by leaving the smaller western fishing circuits. However, I gained the opportunity to make it big on the national level on the BASSMASTER Tournament Trail. Now, the best bass fishermen in the country awaited me. And so did the unfamiliar lakes.

LIFE WAS CHANGING RAPIDLY AND GETTING MORE COMPLICATED BY THE DAY. I MUST ADMIT, JILL AND I WENT THROUGH SOME CULTURE SHOCK.

Life was changing rapidly and getting more complicated by the day. I must admit, Jill and I went through some culture shock when we moved to rural East Texas. The people were friendly in East Texas, and we had a few friends in the area already. However, in the small towns things move at a slower pace. There were no malls and no chain restaurants. Even the United States Post Office didn't service our area! We had a Post Office Box in the "metropolis" of Jasper twenty minutes away.

Our move also put us in a place averaging 50 inches of rain per year. I can tell you some weird sounds were coming from Sam Rayburn Lake on warm summer evenings. I don't know if the legendary stories about 20-pound bullfrogs are real, but these bullfrogs sounded every bit of that. Overall, I have fond memories of living right on the shores of "Big Sam."

New Season, New Start

The new season started in September of 1990. I was not about to leave Jill behind in a strange place all alone, so she hit the road with me that fall. The first tournament was back on the St. Lawrence River in New York. I had bombed out there before at the first season's opener, but I was hoping my performance would improve as I became more familiar with the St. Lawrence and other fishing stops. I finished ninth that time and thought I was off to a much better start in my second year as a pro.

Unfortunately, that would turn out to be my highest finish during that year. I placed in the money in only four of the ten

BASSMASTER tournaments that year. My other money finishes were between twentieth and fiftieth place. That made for a rather lean year financially. I had won perhaps $12,000 with expenses at around $50,000. However, I did qualify for the 1991 BASSMASTERS Classic that season. I was one of the last guys to qualify, but I was in!

FROM A COMPETITIVE STANDPOINT, I WAS A COMPLETE BASKETCASE WHEN JILL AND I FLEW INTO BALTIMORE THE FOLLOWING MONTH FOR MY FIRST CLASSIC.

Making your first BASSMASTERS Classic is a huge deal for a bass pro since it is the biggest annual event in freshwater fishing in the world. Everybody who is anybody in the fishing industry is there. The Classic is the best place to display your talents and make a name for yourself. I knew qualifying for the "Big Show" would add a lot of credibility to my career as a professional.

Jill and I were married on July 6, 1991 at St. James Episcopal Church, in Lincoln City, Oregon. Lots of family and friend attended our beautiful fairytale wedding on the Oregon coast. For my bachelor party, we chartered a boat for twelve in the coastal port of Depoe Bay and went salmon fishing in the Pacific Ocean. We had a big rehearsal dinner party with fresh grilled salmon that evening at Fogarty Creek State Park, right on the beach. Jill and I then headed off to the Inn at Otter Crest for our honeymoon. Our room overlooked the Pacific, and we could watch whales and sea lions from our balcony.

From a competitive standpoint, I was a complete basketcase when Jill and I flew into Baltimore the following month for my first Classic. I got involved in all the hype and hoopla and found myself thinking about everything else except what the fish were doing. I was having so much fun at the pre-tournament events, going to fancy dinner parties and meeting new people, I really didn't focus on the job at hand.

In fact, I didn't even have time to carry my rods, reels, and tackle boxes down to the boat yard the night before the first practice day on the Chesapeake Bay. As we went to bed the evening before the first day of practice, I asked Jill to set the alarm clock and ordered a wake-up call just in case. When the alarm clock went off, I instinctively jumped out of bed and got dressed. I felt a little tired, but the adrenaline was soon pumping. I threw on my tournament jersey, grabbed my rods, tackle box, and life jacket, and I headed across the deserted lobby. "Where was everybody?" I wondered. I felt so proud of myself—I had a jump on everybody already!

I LEFT THE HOTEL AND WALKED THREE BLOCKS TO THE BOAT YARD, MENTALLY REHEARSING MY PLAN OF ATTACK. I WAS IN THE CLASSIC, BABY, AND I WAS GOING FISHIN'!

I left the hotel and walked three blocks to the boat yard, mentally rehearsing my plan of attack. Suddenly some rough-looking kids appeared in the shadows on the corner, but they just gave me a strange look as I lugged my stuff down the sidewalk. I even heard them snickering after I passed by, but I didn't care. I was in the Classic, baby, and I was going fishin'! When I finally made it to the empty boatyard, reality began to hit me. Confused, I asked the security guard, "Where is everyone?" He just chuckled and said, "You're a little early, aren't you?" I looked at my watch for the first time— it was 12:45 a.m.! Jill laughed about her joke the rest of the week.

Soul-Searching

I had a lot of fun at that first Classic, but I fished terribly in the tournament, finishing thirty-sixth out of forty fishermen. When the festivities ended, I went back to reality. I had lost a lot of money my first two years on the BASSMASTER Tour. My big gamble didn't exactly pay off as handsomely as I anticipated. I spent all the money I had saved from my tournament success out West, and when I entered my third full season on the BASSMASTER Tour, the coffers were empty.

Focus

Determined to become the best fisherman I could be, I searched for every possible edge I could find to make me a better fisherman. I didn't understand why I wasn't finding the success on the the Tour that I had experienced out west. Was I doing everything I possibly could to succeed? Had I lost my focus? What was I was missing? It was time for some soul searching.

I had heard some talk from a few of the top pros of the day. They said in order for someone to be his best, a fisherman must address the full man: body, soul, and spirit. I had the first two down pat—I was an athletic guy who put his soul into everything he ever did. That spiritual part really caught my attention. I had not incorporated spirituality into my "fishing formula for success." I figured it was worth a shot to see if this was the missing link in my career.

DETERMINED TO BECOME THE BEST FISHERMAN I COULD BE, I SEARCHED FOR EVERY POSSIBLE EDGE I COULD FIND TO MAKE ME A BETTER FISHERMAN. IT WAS TIME FOR SOME SOUL SEARCHING.

I then set out on a spiritual journey. Outside of that perplexing dream about my dad years ago, I didn't know the first thing about the spiritual realm, although I had an instinctive notion it was real. I was curious, and it wasn't long before I was browsing the Religious and New Age aisles at a Barnes and Noble bookstore. I was surprised at the vast amount of material I found on different ideas concerning spirituality. I didn't know where to begin.

I guess you could say I had a narrow worldview up to that point. My world consisted of fishing, sports, and my new bride, Jill. I didn't hang around spiritual people. Whatever I couldn't find in the sports page wasn't important to me. So on the first steps of my spiritual journey I just looked to some of the top fishermen of the day who claimed to have a handle on spiritual issues. A few of them were really into the New Age movement, which teaches that people have an unlimited inner power. It focuses on tapping into that power. Some of the top pros had been quite successful with this mindset, and I figured that if it worked for them it would work for me too. They had this spiritual stuff dialed in as far as I could tell. Their tournament records sure were impressive anyway. I started reading some stuff by authors they recommended like Richard Bach and Tom Brown in hopes of finding a competitive edge. Most of it was New Age ideology, and I immediately liked it.

MY WORLD CONSISTED OF FISHING, SPORTS, AND MY NEW BRIDE, JILL. WHATEVER I COULDN'T FIND IN THE SPORTS PAGE WASN'T IMPORTANT.

I learned I was in control of my own destiny. If I wanted to be more successful, all I had to do was look inside. What an adrenalin rush! I read more books and continued to feed my ego a steady diet of New Age ideology.

Something's Wrong

When my third season on the BASSMASTER Tour was about to begin, Jill and I were broke. We agreed she would stay home and get a job to help make ends meet. So after getting married in July and "attending" (I wouldn't call it fishing) my first Classic in August, our summer-long party was about to end. The familiar refrains of "Dandy" Don Meredeth singing, "Turn out the Lights, the Party's Over," kept echoing in my head. By September, I was off on the tournament trail again, and Jill stayed in Sam Rayburn waiting tables at a restaurant called Dorothy's.

Family

That half-baked arrangement lasted one month. Let's just say that the idea of her staying home alone didn't go over very well. Young husbands, listen up! Do not leave your newlywed wife alone in the middle of nowhere while you travel around the country on business. She will not be happy without you, and she may not be happy with you when you return! Jill had not been around that area long enough to establish any real friendships. I had taken her far away from her family out West and left her all alone.

We were too much in love to spend much time apart and decided we would be a team. Jill desired to travel with me and support me in everything I did—it's what we both wanted. As long as the team could afford to stay on the Tour, we both would. If the day came when the team couldn't afford to fish any longer, we would both find something else to do. That was the right decision. It was the best thing for our marriage.

I did a little better my third year on the BASSMASTER Tour—breaking even for the first time instead of losing money. I even picked up a few more sponsors. Yet I was nowhere near my potential. I "made the money" (earning a top fifty finish) in half of the tournaments I fished that third year. However, even with my best finish that year at fourth place, the rest of my money finishes were low.

I also qualified for my second Classic in Birmingham, Alabama that year, but I didn't improve much over my first performance. In Birmingham, I finished thirty-fourth—only a slight improvement from the year before in Baltimore. I had blamed my poor finish in Baltimore on being caught up in all the excitement. However, after a similar finish in Birmingham, I had no excuse. Something was missing.

> I HAD BLAMED MY POOR FINISH IN BALTIMORE ON BEING CAUGHT UP IN ALL THE EXCITEMENT. HOWEVER, AFTER A SIMILAR FINISH IN BIRMINGHAM, I HAD NO EXCUSE. SOMETHING WAS MISSING. I WASN'T LIVING UP TO MY POTENTIAL, AND I KNEW IT.

I wasn't living up to my potential, and I knew it. I was starting to get concerned. Previously, every time I had taken on a new challenge in my fishing career, I had conquered it within two years. I was not even close to conquering the BASSMASTER challenge, even after three years. I had lost money the first two years of my new endeavor, and I improved in my third year only enough to break even. I wasn't utilizing my talent the way I should have been at that point, and my career wasn't the

Giving

only thing falling flat. My relationships were souring as well. Jill and I were having some rocky times during our first few years of marriage. Everything was turning out to be harder than I anticipated.

Meanwhile, I had turned into a selfish individual who traveled around the country doing something I loved without giving a rip about anyone or anything else. I had not contributed anything to society, and that was starting to bother me. Sure, I was still chasing my dream, but that was all it was: my dream. I cared solely about myself. My world revolved around two things: me, and how many bass I caught. Fishing was my god—I sacrificed my time and my talents at its feet. Yet when all you care about is yourself, and at the same time you have begun to despise the person you are, life isn't too grand. I was beginning to question all of the talk saying we are in control of our own destiny. I was in control, but I sure wasn't reaching my destiny.

I inventoried what was going on in my life. As far as I could tell, I was doing all the right things. I had the same mindset I'd had in my prior glory years out West. I worked hard, I was focused, I was still passionate about fishing, and I was devoted to Jill. I was doing everything in my power to make my world the wonderful place I wanted it to be— the world my New Age spirituality was promising me. I was doing everything in the natural realm I could to have the life I wanted to have, but without results. I felt like I was running in quicksand.

After my personal inventory came up short, I determined the only thing left was the spiritual realm. I had always

I HAD TURNED INTO A SELFISH INDIVIDUAL WHO TRAVELED AROUND THE COUNTRY DOING SOMETHING I LOVED WITHOUT GIVING A RIP ABOUT ANYONE OR ANYTHING ELSE. MY WORLD REVOLVED AROUND TWO THINGS: ME, AND HOW MANY BASS I CAUGHT.

felt the spiritual world was very real, but I could never get my arms around it. My few brief encounters with it, like when I had the dream about my dad having cancer, whet my appetite to probe deeper. I knew answers were out there; I just had to find them.

Something Has to Change

As I began my fourth season on the Tour in the fall of 1992, I explored the spiritual realm in search of answers. My main motivation was to discover a fishing formula for success, not necessarily to change my own heart. I felt frighteningly incomplete as a person, but I felt more of a responsibility to find the answer for my career. I plowed into the New Age stuff with abandon, hoping to turn it around.

JILL WALKED INTO OUR DEN ONCE BEFORE A TOURNAMENT TO FIND ME SITTING CROSS-LEGGED ON THE FLOOR, TRYING TO CHANNEL TO A "COMPLETE STATE OF NOTHINGNESS." I COULDN'T DO IT, AND I FELT FOOLISH FOR TRYING.

I got into chanting, channeling, and transcendental meditation. Jill, trying to support me in my quest for success, read the same kind of material I did. She became interested in palm reading and Indian spirits. She even saw a Shaman, a spirit guide. Shamans claim to affect someone on the soul level by walking both worlds of the physical and spiritual, speaking with ancestors, animals, nature, and spirits to bring back helpful information.

We surrounded ourselves with whatever might help us center on our spirituality, including medicine bags, dream-catchers and other paraphernalia. Jill walked into our den once before a tournament to find me sitting cross-legged on the floor, trying to channel to a "complete state of nothingness." I couldn't do it, and I felt foolish trying.

Even though we were caught up in New Age spirituality, at the same time something began pulling us back to our roots. I had grown up in the Episcopal church, and Jill had grown up

Catholic. When I wasn't on tour, Jill and I started attending church back home in Jasper, Texas. There was a spiritual battle raging around my family. Our souls were in a tug-of-war, and we were miserable.

Oh, taste and see that the Lord is good.
Blessed is the man who trusts in Him.

—Psalm 34:8 (NKJV)

Chapter Five

RESCUED

Earlier the previous spring, an article had come out in a college magazine about New Age professional fishermen and their philosophical differences with Christian professional anglers. I read the article and was disappointed with how the New Age pros ridiculed the director of FOCAS, Terry Chupp, and other Christian pros. In contrast, they glorified themselves, even featuring a picture of a pro fishing naked in his boat. Not only were they running down good men, these guys were glorifying themselves to an extreme. I've learned anytime you try to glorify yourself at others' expense, it pushes people away.

The more I got to know these New Agers, the more I began to realize that I didn't see anything in these guys' lives that I connected with, other than the fact they did so well in fishing tournaments. "If their spirituality was the real deal," I wondered, "Why wasn't that transforming them into someone I wanted to be like?"

That was a dangerous time for me. I had set off on a spiritual journey without the Truth as my guide. It was like trying to navigate across an ocean with the wrong map. I got lost, and it affected every area of my life. I was not living up to my potential in my relationships, at home or at the workplace.

For example, my relationships with Jill and others weren't improving; in fact they had taken a downturn. Although Jill and I had a good marriage, we experienced many hard times with no lasting peace or joy. I had exposed myself and my family to what I later learned was the occult. We were in the middle of spiritual warfare. Someone or something didn't want us to discover the

Jill and I visited Maui while in the islands to see my parents over Christmas in 1989.

truth about this short-changed spirituality. For example, whenever Jill would pick up a Bible on occasion to read it, she would suddenly get a headache, blurring her vision so she couldn't read it anymore. It was strange. In fact, when Jill and I would try to get up and go to church, we'd often get into terrible fights on the way there, usually over something stupid. In the heat of the moment, I'd slam on my brakes and turn the car around to go home, skipping church altogether.

My fourth year on the BASSMASTER Tour started out with a bang as I finished second on the Potomac River in Maryland in September of 1992. I saw a brief glimmer of hope that I might be onto something with my renewed focus on the New Age ideology. However, those high hopes began to fizzle later in the season. My tournament success, which was supposed to benefit from my new spiritual journey, was suffering immensely. After two years of trying to tap into my unlimited potential through the New Age movement, I was not getting any better as a fisherman. In fact, I was struggling badly.

Things came to a head on Christmas night 1992. At home in our bed that night, Jill and I simultaneously woke up at 2:00 a.m. in a cold sweat, shaking with fear. The fact that something had woken both of us out of a sound sleep proved to us it wasn't in our imaginations. We immediately sensed a terrible, evil presence in our house. Imagine if an axe murderer broke into your house and you could hear him coming down the hall toward your room to kill you—it was that frightening. Jill and I lay there in bed scared to death. Fear permeated our home.

Thinking at first it might be a robber, we got up and turned on all the lights, but found no one there. There were no signs of forced entry, and nothing was missing. We sat down in the living room, relieved there was no one there. However, the terrifying sensation remained and grew even stronger. We both realized then that this presence was not physical, but spiritual.

We returned to our bedroom and both lay in bed frightened by something we could not see. It was the only time in my life where I have experienced something this horrifying. We were both still shaking. We didn't know what was happening, but we confirmed each other's feelings—this evil presence in our home was not leaving. Jill had an idea. She quickly pushed aside the incense and meditation candles on our bedside table to uncover an old, dust-covered Bible. She opened it at random and began to read it aloud. The evil presence left immediately!

Courage

WE IMMEDIATELY SENSED A TERRIBLE, EVIL PRESENCE IN OUR HOUSE. IMAGINE IF AN AXE MURDERER BROKE INTO YOUR HOUSE AND YOU COULD HEAR HIM COMING... IT WAS THAT FRIGHTENING.

As we reflected on what had just taken place, we began to realize that the evil presence in our home was further proof of just how real the spiritual realm was. We understood that there were two spiritual forces at work in the world: good and evil. For the first time in my life, I experienced the power of God firsthand. The power in the Word of God blew me away. When Jill opened that old dust-covered Bible, it was just like someone threw on a light switch in the room. The darkness left that fast. We had never experienced anything like that before and haven't since.

Ironically, when we told our New Age friends and mentors about our freaky experience, they saw it as a sort of spiritual promotion. "You're now ready to go on to the next level in your journey," they encouraged us. I wanted no part of that "next level." In fact, I was beginning to feel the New Age philosophy had no place in my life.

Professionally, I wasn't getting anywhere in fishing, which is why I became involved in the New Age movement in the first place. For three and a half years, I toiled on the BASSMASTER Tour, and I could never reach my goals. I tried everything I knew to do, and none of it was good enough to be successful on the Tour. In February of 1993, I capped off a horrific run during the middle of my fourth season with the worst tournament of my career, the BASSMASTER Georgia Top 100 at Lake Seminole. I blanked the last two days of that four-day event and finished just about dead last in the field. I had hit bottom with my fishing. However, that tournament also became the backdrop for a major change in my life. I wasn't coming close to my potential as a fisherman. I could feel that whatever was wrong was somehow tied to my spiritual pursuit; I was going down the wrong path.

A Life Change

Adding it all up, I had to ask, "Why continue in this New Age stuff?" I'd already given it two years with no lasting results. I no longer had an appetite for learning about New Age ideology. Instead of bringing vitality to my life, it was more like outdated spoiled milk that needed tossing out.

I decided to bail out and try to find the real truth somewhere else. My dad was still suffering through his bout with cancer, forcing me to face the very real threat that he could die. My own mortality haunted me daily as I struggled to get a handle on all that was going on around me and to bring God into focus. I had never spent too much time thinking about God, but when I had, He was a distant concept to me. Now I began to draw on the only Christianity I knew—the limited church background I had as a child, the little time we spent at the Episcopal church in Jasper, and even a bit of preaching I caught on television from time to time.

From my early experience with church, I knew the Christmas story and the Easter story and had even learned the facts about

Jesus' life. But no one told me as a young adult that God wanted me to pursue a personal relationship with Him, so I didn't. I carried all those facts about Christianity around in my head with me, but I never knew I could have a personal relationship with God. To me, God was a Sunday morning ritual I left behind when I walked out of church on Sunday morning.

However, now I was beginning to hear about a concept that was new to me. God loved me and wanted me to love Him and pursue a personal relationship with Him through faith in His son, Jesus Christ. At first I didn't understand, even though I had gone to church for most of my life, but it was the message of the Gospel. I would soon learn there is a big difference between knowing about Jesus and having a personal relationship with Him. Contrary to popular belief, just going to church doesn't cut it. Many people think anyone who goes to church is a Christian. This is not true. Churches are full of people who don't know Jesus; and I was one of them. For the first time, I began to sense that I had finally encountered the truth.

CHURCHES ARE FULL OF PEOPLE WHO DON'T KNOW JESUS; AND I WAS ONE OF THEM. FOR THE FIRST TIME, I BEGAN TO SENSE THAT I HAD FINALLY ENCOUNTERED THE TRUTH.

Jill and I began to understand more of what the Bible says about the reality of the spiritual realm and the nature of good and evil. What a revelation! Jill caught on to the truth more quickly than I did. In fact, she accepted Jesus as her Lord and Savior a few weeks before I did and began fervently praying for me to make the same discovery. She had never fasted before, but she even fasted during my tournament in Georgia, praying God would open my eyes. God answered her prayers.

I really opened up to God after I attended my first FOCAS meeting during that devastating tournament in Georgia. I walked into the meeting a desperate man, so aware of my shortcomings and ready to hand my life over to someone or something that could save me from the mess I was in. Terry Chupp, the man who first talked to me about Christ three years before, shared during the meeting how to become a Christian, and my heart burned with a desire to experience a relationship with the one true God. I had tried so hard on my own to tap into my unlimited potential, and I could not do it. I was tired and frustrated at driving my own life and decided it was time to hand the reigns over. I humbly confessed the fact that I was a sinner and repented for ignoring God and trying to do it all on my own. I released the whole load and gave it to God to handle for me.

Driving home from the tournament later that week, Jill and I shared a tender time together as I prayed aloud with her to surrender my life to Jesus and accept Him as my Lord and Savior. That moment on February 28, 1993, is so real in my memory I can recall it like it was yesterday.

Salvation 101

Christianity is based on the principle that God himself became manifest in the flesh in His Son Jesus Christ. He lived a perfect sinless life and humbled himself in such a way that he was crucified on a cross, died, and was buried. After three days, He rose from the dead, ascended into Heaven, and is alive today. Why did God do this? He loves us so much that He wanted to provide a way for us to spend eternity with Him! To do this, we just need to confess that Jesus Christ is Lord and believe in our hearts that God raised Him from the dead and that He is alive today.

So, how did I actually take the leap and become a Christian? That part was easy. Romans 10:9-10 says, "If you confess with your mouth, 'Jesus is Lord,' and believe in your heart that God raised Him from the dead, you will be saved. For it is with your heart that you believe and are justified, and it is with your mouth that you confess and are saved." If we will wholeheartedly repent of all our sins and if we believe by faith that Jesus Christ is God's Son, God will forgive our sins and will welcome us into an eternal relationship with Him.

When I prayed with Jill driving home that day from Georgia, I said something like:

God, I know I am a sinner, but I know that you love me. I ask You to forgive me my sins. I believe in Jesus Christ, that He died on the cross as payment for my sins, and that He rose from the grave and is alive today. I ask You to enter my life right now and help me to live for You. I pray this in Jesus' name. Amen.

There is no long list of good things we must do or of bad things we must abstain from doing. No matter how many "good" deeds we do, we still won't be good enough for God on our own. Yet, if we remain in our sinful humanity, we will die and spend eternity separated from God. Romans 6:23 teaches, "For the wages of sin is death, but the gift of God is eternal life in Christ Jesus our Lord." None of us is perfect. We all fall short of the standard that is Jesus Christ. Romans 3:23 says, "For all have sinned and fall short of the glory of God."

So, why should a pure, righteous, and perfect God accept a dirty, rotten sinner like me into His Kingdom for eternity? God understands our human condition, and He has mercy on us. Most importantly, He loves us more than we can imagine. "But God demonstrates His own love for us in this: While we were still sinners, Christ died for us," (Romans 5:8). Understanding how perfect and righteous God really is enlightened me. Jesus was the perfect, sinless man. He was holy, pure, and just. When you meet Him one day when this life is over, the awesome holy presence He carries will just blow you away. His promise is a simple one: "And everyone who calls on the name of the Lord will be saved," (Acts 2:21).

I WAS AMAZED AT HOW GOD CHANGED MY HEART ONCE I HUMBLY PRAYED TO RECEIVE CHRIST AS MY LORD AND SAVIOR. HE DIDN'T DEMAND THAT I CLEAN UP MY ACT BEFORE I CAME TO HIM.

I was amazed at how God changed my heart once I humbly prayed to receive Christ as my Lord and Savior. He didn't demand that I clean up my act before I came to him; rather, he accepted me right where I was and began to change my heart. He made me want to do the right thing. He convinced me that His way is the better way. He changed me from the inside out. This inner transformation is what many Christians refer to as being "born again" since it's like starting over in life.

Everything Changes

Family

And start over I did! My life dramatically changed in every way. For the first time in my life I knew what it was like to have a God-centered marriage. My wife and I were both lost for so long because we didn't know how to live other than to follow the ways of the world. We were living together and traveling together to my tournaments eleven months before we were married. If I could do it differently, I would. That lifestyle did not line up with what I learned God wanted in our relationship. Putting God in the middle of our marriage gave it new life. We were happily married before, but we had missed out on so much. Our moments of joy and peace seemed so fleeting. Our marriage was built on a shaky foundation—ourselves. We noticed a dramatic change for the better once we prioritized God as the foundation of our relationship. We began praying together and going to church—this time without fighting all the way to worship service!

FOR THE FIRST TIME IN MY LIFE, I KNEW WHAT IT WAS LIKE TO HAVE A GOD-CENTERED MARRIAGE. PUTTING GOD IN THE MIDDLE OF OUR MARRIAGE GAVE IT NEW LIFE.

When we saw the light of God's truth, the darkness surrounding our old lifestyle horrified us. We totally cleaned house. We got rid of all our new age books and music. We must have trashed hundreds of CD's and tapes, paintings and artwork. We knew instinctively they had to go. We loved our old friends who were not believers, but we realized we needed to make new friends who would encourage our fledg-

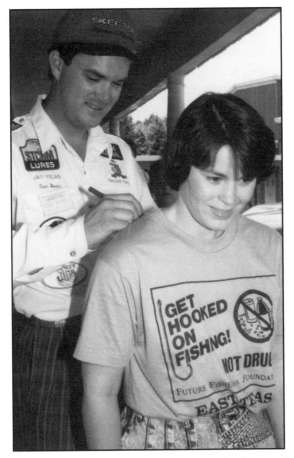

Signing autographs at the East Texas "Get Hooked on Fishing Not on Drugs" tournament event in the early nineties.

ling faith. We were just babes, so to speak, "newbies" to Christianity who made a lot of mistakes. We didn't necessarily do everything the right way. In retrospect we could have been more loving and considerate to some of our old friends. I see now that leaving them bitter and confused was no way to lead them to the same wonderful discovery we had made. In fact, it probably turned them off to the whole thing.

We became very involved in a church called Life Tabernacle, in Jasper. Like most churches in Jasper, it was a very small church, but it was exactly what I needed at the time. What some might call a full-gospel church, Life Tabernacle believed in the laying on of hands, speaking in tongues, and a world of other charismatic practices. I took in the whole thing, believing by faith everything in the Bible and all God had for us. I totally immersed myself in my relationship with Christ and began growing rapidly. I wanted it all. I didn't want some watered down cultural version of Christianity.

Giving

I went to church every time the doors opened, driving 40 miles round trip several times during the week. Our church began having a morning prayer time five days a week at 6:00 a.m. I was there bright and early, eager to learn how to pray alongside other Christians. We began tithing to that little church, giving 10 percent of our income, and often much more, as an act of worship. We had worship videos or Christian tapes going all the time at the house. We were wide open on this deal. I jumped into Christianity headlong just like I'd done with everything in my life. I wanted to be the best Christian I could be.

I JUMPED INTO CHRISTIANITY HEADLONG JUST LIKE I'D DONE WITH EVERYTHING IN MY LIFE. I WANTED TO BE THE BEST CHRISTIAN I COULD BE.

After about six months in that church, we began visiting Tanglewood Baptist in Jasper and then some larger churches in Lufkin, Texas. We attended Word of Life, a non-denominational church pastored by a godly man named Simon Purvis. We also visited Lufkin Assembly, a wonderful Assembly of God church where a young man named Todd Hudnall was pastor. Jill and I really started to grow spiritually in these churches. We were like big sponges, soaking up everything we could about the Christian faith. We eventually stopped church-hopping and settled down in the church where God wanted us to serve, and we have been in the same church ever since.

The transformation in my career was incredible. My frustrating downturn immediately reversed, and my career unexpectedly blasted off like a rocket. Everything changed for the better in the next two and a half years. I placed in the top ten in seventeen out of the next thirty-four BASSMASTER tournaments. My phenomenal run from the time of my salvation in February 1993 to June 1995 rivals the best hot streak any fisherman has ever had. The Lord blessed me with my first win in the 1993 BASSMASTER Top 100 on the Potomac River in Maryland and culminated my run with the June 1995 win at the BASSMASTERS Superstars tournament on the Illinois River in Peoria, Illinois. That Superstars win was the highlight of my pro career up to that point. Back in the mid '90s, Superstars was the second biggest tournament in the country each year, second only to the BASS-MASTERS Classic. What a thrill it was to take my first victory lap around a coliseum carrying the American Flag, with Jill sitting by my side.

I believe that once I surrendered to Jesus and His Lordship, I became a man God could use for His glory. Immediately after I

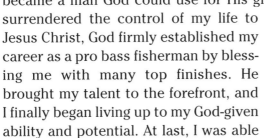

Courage

surrendered the control of my life to Jesus Christ, God firmly established my career as a pro bass fisherman by blessing me with many top finishes. He brought my talent to the forefront, and I finally began living up to my God-given ability and potential. At last, I was able to reach the top of my game.

HOW IRONIC THAT MY FISHING SUCCESS FINALLY CAME WHEN I QUIT TRYING. I SIMPLY SOUGHT GOD AND I TRIED TO BE OBEDIENT. HE TOOK CARE OF THE REST.

How ironic that my fishing success finally came when I quit trying. I simply sought God and tried to be obedient. He took care of the rest. I had struggled under my own power for over three and a half years trying to make it in this sport as a top pro. I could not do it. Then I met Jesus and completely surrendered my life to Him. And what a sweet surrender it was. I didn't surrender as part of a fishing formula looking to get something out of the deal; I surrendered because I realized who Jesus Christ really was, fell in love with Him, and longed for Him to be my Lord and Savior.

It is important to note that I didn't come to God looking to "make a deal." I didn't come to God and say, "I'll do this for you if you'll bless my fishing career." When He revealed Himself to

YOU CAN'T MANIPULATE GOD. THERE ARE NO GUARANTEES. GOD HAS A PLAN THAT IS INDIVIDUAL TO YOU, AND IT MAY NOT BE WHAT YOU EXPECT.

me in all His love, holiness, power, majesty, and authority, I was simply in awe. The fact that He has blessed my fishing has nothing to do with how much I love Him. If I never caught another bass the rest of my life, it wouldn't affect my relationship with God one bit.

You can't manipulate God. An aspiring pro who reads what happened to me can't assume just because he gets saved that his fishing career will take off as a result. There are no guarantees. You should come to God because a relationship with Him is worth it on its own. He is awesome! If it's His will for your fishing to succeed, then God can help establish you as a winner. God has a plan that is individual to you, and it may not be what you expect. You have to remember, God's will is for every person from all walks of life to give Him glory for everything, win or lose. Giving God credit for success should be a natural reflex for anyone when good things happen, not something reserved for athletes and professionals to do in front of the media.

Work Ethic

From a fishing perspective, my first two and a half years as a Christian were definitely exciting. I still kept working just as hard as I had before. I still had the burning desire and the passionate hunger that I'd possessed earlier in my career. Those things did not go away. God just made it all complete. He was what I had been missing. No soul is ever complete without coming into a relationship with Almighty God, our Creator. We can't be complete without Him.

The formal awards banquet was one of the things I enjoyed most, though, about that Superstars win. The mayor of Peoria was so touched by the Christian testimony I shared on the victory platform that he sang a song in my honor in front of hundreds at the banquet. What a surprise! He sang, "Let it Begin With Me," a song about how we can make a difference with our lives and help to make the world a better place. I have been to many awards banquets but have never seen anyone, let alone a dignitary, sing the victor a song. Afterwards, the mayor encouraged me to keep sharing God's love everywhere I went.

My experiences as a born-again Christian proved to me that New Age ideas about directing your own destiny lead nowhere. It is seductive because it initially produces a huge adrenaline rush, making you feel empowered—in control of your life. It tells you that your life will be whatever you want it to be. The devil wants us to believe that we are in control of our destiny because that fills us with pride. Pride is the number one thing that keeps people from a relationship with Jesus, and it played a significant role in hindering my spiritual and professional growth. Proverbs 14:12 says, "There is a way that seems right to a man, but its end is the way of death," (NKJV). That perfectly sums up the New Age movement to me. In contrast, Jesus said in John 10:10, "I have come that they may have life, and that they may have it more abundantly," (NKJV).

PRIDE IS THE NUMBER ONE THING THAT KEEPS PEOPLE FROM A RELATIONSHIP WITH JESUS, AND IT PLAYED A SIGNIFICANT ROLE IN HINDERING MY SPIRITUAL AND PROFESSIONAL GROWTH.

I have not been able to maintain the same success that I did in my first couple of years as a Christian. Nobody in the history of this sport has been able to keep that level of performance up forever. I had finished in the top ten in half of the tournaments I fished for a thirty-month period. I believe that was just a season in my life where God, by His Grace, decided to establish me as a top bass pro. It was only the first part in a much bigger plan. I had committed my ways to Him, and I was now a vessel He could use to further His kingdom. He took that period of time to establish my name among the sport's elite for His Glory, both then and in the future.

God transformed my fishing career, giving me a platform from which I could share His love with other fishermen. As soon as I became a Christian, I started sharing my testimony at churches and FOCAS meetings to tell others about my dramatic

Giving

experience. I loved sharing my testimony because it was a chance to share with others what God had done in my life.

Desire Comes Full Circle

After becoming a Christian I no longer had the burning desire to win just for the sake of beating everyone else. Instead of driving myself to be the top bass pro, my desire became to serve the kingdom of God.

I started by putting God first, and I stopped seeing fishing as my god. I became a better husband to my wife and, later, a great dad to my kids. Fishing took a backseat to my relationships with my family. I also began serving the kingdom by sharing the love of Christ with the fishermen of America. That was my consuming passion and still is. God knows that keeping these priorities will bring us true peace and joy. He loves us so much that He is always looking out for our best interests. He wants our lives to be rich and full so he changes our hearts and resets our priorities. I knew if I could do these things then I would be able to consider myself a successful man.

I STARTED PUTTING GOD FIRST, AND I STOPPED SEEING FISHING AS MY GOD. I BECAME A BETTER HUSBAND TO MY WIFE AND, LATER, A GREAT DAD TO MY KIDS.

Am I saying I suddenly became perfect? No way. But my heart's desire was to be a godly man. I still messed up and made mistakes every day. However, when I fell short, God forgave me, lifted me back up, and encouraged me to try again. I was only just beginning my lifelong walk with Christ. I had a lot of maturing to do and had so much to learn. I still need this help today and always will.

The only thing we will leave behind that matters is our legacy. The only important thing about a legacy is the kind of impact we had on other people. Did we positively influence others, or did we negatively influence them? Did our lives help make

Giving

the lives of others better or worse? This is all that will matter. We can bring a little sunshine into other people's lives in many ways. But after experiencing God the way I have, I am fully persuaded that the absolute best thing we can do for others is to share God's love with them and help lead them into a relationship with Him.

My win at the '95 Superstars event was the final page on that "post salvation" success chapter in my life. God had established me as a top bass pro. However, the seasons of life and the changes they bring never cease to amaze me, and the next few years proved to be a season of spiritual growth and maturity.

Trials and tribulations did a lot more to improve me as a person than success ever did.

—A key observation while I was maturing into a champion.

Even in the beginning, there was no such thing as too many fish!

O.K., so it's not a bass. I caught this 30-pound Chinook Salmon in Oregon on the Siletz River in 1983.

I purchased my first boat in 1984—a 1968 14' Smokercraft, powered by a 9.9 horsepower outboard. Painted yellow, and on a rusted trailer, it perfectly coordinated with my old, rusted Volkswagen Rabbit I drove all through college.

My high school buddy and roommate in college, Brad Sharpton, in front of his house after college graduation. Having left the Smokercraft for a Skeeter, I've got my boat, and I'm ready to turn pro.

My mentor and friend, Bill Sedar, enjoying a day on Lake Cachuma in 1996—his weekly fishing haunt for the past 42 years.

President George Bush, Sr. competed on another team during Ray Scott's 1993 Eagles of Angling Bass Tournament in Montgomery, Alabama. Shown looking on as we weigh our fish are Ray Scott, founder of the Bass Anglers Sportsman's Society, President Bush, me, and my good friend Jeff Barnes.

Jill and I posing on some driftwood at our wedding reception, July 6, 1991 on the windy Oregon Coast.

Jill and I celebrating our first Christmas together. In 1991, my world consisted of Jill and fishing. We had no idea how our lives would change.

Ray Scott talks to me and Jill about my first BASSMASTERS win in September 1993. This was in the middle of my hot-streak after Jill and I became Christians earlier that year. My phenomenal run from the time of my salvation in February 1993 to June 1995 rivals the best hot streak any fisherman ever had.

Ray Scott, sans his famous cowboy hat, congratulates me after my 1995 Superstars win. For two-and-a-half years leading up to this win, I finished in the top 10 in half of the BASSMASTERS events I fished.

Jimmy Houston, pro fisherman and TV personality, pauses for a photo with Jill and me at a dinner party at the 1996 BASSMASTERS Classic.

Big sister, Hannah, and me at Bethany's birth. I never knew how much fun fatherhood could be!

Having special times with my family is a top priority. Here, we're posing for an outdoor writer who accompanied us on an outing when we lived near Sam Rayburn Lake in Texas.

My dad, Joe, and I out for a round of golf together.

Weighing-in during the first FLW Tournament of the 2002 season at Lake Okeechobee. Not only did I have a unique, carefree mindset going into the first tournament in January, this tournament marked a milestone in my spiritual journey.

The family joins me down on the boat dock for a weigh-in during the FLW tournament season. Their support means so much to me on the road.

Hannah, my oldest daughter, is always ready for the camera! Posing with Dad at Lake Champlain, June 2002.

Dave Lonsberry of Kellogg's congratulates me on my 2002 Wal-Mart FLW Angler of the Year award. Going into that final tournament on Lake Champlain, I was in second place for the title, but I was 28 points behind Kevin Van Dam.

Every day during the 2002 CITGO BASSMASTERS Classic, the Alabama Power Company would generate water from Logan Martin Dam from 10:00 a.m. until 3:00 p.m. I was fishing 500 yards below the dam on the last good ambush points heading upriver before the dam.

Showing my game-face on the 30-mile run to my fishing area during the 2002 Classic.

Landing my first keeper on the final day of the 2002 Classic.

The final day crowd at the 2002 Classic—around 18,000 bass fans from all over the country. It's electrifying!

At the weigh-in, each pro brings in his catch and puts it in a basket. The results from the digital scale are then displayed for the audience to see.

I was excited to land the biggest bass each day of the 2002 Classic.

Being congratulated by some of the Skeeter pro staff and employees after my 2002 Classic win.

This was no dream. After 15 years of pro bass fishing, I had earned the title of World Champion!

Hoisting a 40-pound trophy overhead while fireworks are exploding all around! The Final Awards show was phenomenal, designed by the same folks who did the closing ceremony at the 2002 Winter Olympics.

Everyone's all smiles at Skeeter! Some of the pro staff and employees after the final weigh-in, hanging together at the Classic Outdoor Show.

Faithful fans lined up after the Classic win for my autograph at the Classic Outdoor Show.

I love my fans and I enjoy the times I have to meet them in events like the 2002 Classic. It's fun mingling with fans who are rooting for you everywhere you go.

After the win with fans at the Classic Outdoor Show, signing autographs and posing for pictures.

My friend and fishing buddy, Clay Dyer, celebrating the 2002 Classic win with me. Clay hasn't let the fact that he was born without any limbs (save a right arm that ends at the elbow) stop him from doing what he loves to do. Clay is a fishing machine and an inspiration to me. He never complains about anything. He just looks forward to each new day and each new challenge with eager anticipation.

Chapter Six

MATURING AS A CHAMPION IN LIFE

The 1995 Superstars win was the culmination of two and a half years of phenomenal success. From that point I moved into a new season of my life. The next seven years were about maturing into the man God intended me to be. I had been a Christian now for over two years, but I had a lot more growing up to do. The church word for this process is "sanctification," or growing into the likeness of Jesus Christ. Maturing as a Christian and a champion in life does not happen overnight. God had to wait until I was ready before he could trust me with bigger and better things in my career.

One of the better things came along six months after I won Superstars. Jill gave birth to our first child, Hannah, on January 3, 1996. Oh, what a little beauty she was and still is! I quickly learned what folks meant when they talked about children being a blessing from the Lord. My little Hannah was the apple of my eye. It was awesome to be a dad for the first time! My second daughter, Bethany, was born in 1998, and what a little darling she is! God made Bethany such a beautiful creation. It is amazing how He makes kids from the same parents so different. My girls are uniquely wonderful!

Being a new father was just a part of my life that was growing more complex by the day. I was learning to deal with the success

Hannah, my oldest of two daughters, at the wheel of my boat as a baby. She already has her dad's love for the water and the outdoors!

that I had gained over the last two and a half years. Success definitely changes your life and opens all kinds of new doors. The old saying about how "success has a thousand fathers" is true. When you are successful, everyone wants to be a part of your life. Many are quick to take credit for helping you to get to where you are. You make many new friends and have many new opportunities. The new relationships and opportunities create new demands on your time. The challenge becomes how to fit everything in.

When you are surrounded by success, it is very easy to be content with who you are as a person. When we face struggles, we tend to lean a lot more on the Lord and rely on Him to help us and sustain us through the hard times. Trials and tribulations did a lot more to improve me as a person than success ever did. God seems to love it when we come to Him for help. He longs for an intimate relationship with us, and sometimes the only way He can get our attention is when we fall on hard times. When success surrounds us, we tend to forget about God.

I was growing closer to God by changing and refining my heart to be more like Jesus through various trials. He was also teaching me how to manage my busy life. Yes, I was busier than I had ever been, but it was manageable. One of the greatest things about the Bible is using it as a blueprint for success in life. God loves us all so much that He wants what is best for us. He wants us to be full of love, peace, and joy, and He desires for us to have successful, productive lives that benefit His Kingdom. This is similar to how parents want their kids to be fruitful people who contribute to society. He gives us a model for how to live contented, productive lives in the Bible.

Maturing in Life

I had to learn how to become a champion in my faith and family before God could grow me into an even greater fishing champion. God had established me as a top pro, but I still had a lot of changing to mature into the man He intended me to be. He had big plans for me, but He was putting my fishing success on hold until I matured. I loved God, but my heart was still full of pride and selfishness.

I STILL HAD A LOT OF PRIDE BACK THEN. I STILL WANTED TO BE THE BOSS OF MY LIFE. I WANTED TO CONTROL THINGS AND RUN THINGS MYSELF—A HARD HABIT TO BREAK.

Back in the late '90s, I would publicly give the glory to God after a win, but inwardly I would puff up with pride. For example, after winning at Lake of the Ozarks in Missouri in 1997, I recall humbly thanking God for the win on the victory stand. However, privately on the drive home, I remember thinking to myself, "I am such an awesome fisherman. It's a wonder I don't win more of these tournaments!" I can't believe I thought that! It is rather embarrassing to the man I am today.

I still had a lot of pride back then. I still wanted to be the boss of my life. I wanted to control things and run things for myself—a hard habit to break. I wanted to beat the other top pros for an ego stroke. I was not ready for any more fishing success at the time, and God knew it.

My girls, Hannah and Bethany, catching blue gill on a pond near our house.

For the next seven years, the chart of my fishing success became a flat line. The period of exponential growth was over, and things leveled off for a while. I still made the BASSMASTERS Classic every year, and I would win an event from time to time, but the fireworks were over for the time being. It took me a while to realize there was nothing wrong with this stage in my career. I was adding dimension to my life, improving as a man and as a Christian. One of my favorite scriptures is Romans 8:28, which says, "In all things, God works together for the good of those who love Him, who have been called according to His purpose."

Life Beyond Fishing

This was the life I wanted. I was in my early thirties, and I was living my dream of being a top bass pro, but now I knew life had so much more to offer. During the tournament season I was spending weeks and weeks on the road, fishing every day. I came home from on the road tournaments, and I would need a break from fishing.

I loved spending time with my family. The special times Jill, Hannah, Bethany, and I have had together are written on my heart forever. Intimate family times like vacations, especially when your kids are young, are just about as good as life gets. In addition to being in love with my daughters, I was more in love with my wife than ever. God was changing her into an awesome woman of God, and I was witnessing the transformation. It was pure bliss when the two of us could get away and spend some quality time together.

Family

By God's grace my dad had healed from his cancer, and he was getting back to enjoying life. I looked forward to playing golf and fishing with my dad and with friends. My dad and I spent quite a few evenings curled up on the sofa, each enjoying our own pint of Cherry Garcia® ice cream while we watched a ballgame. I even enjoyed the challenge of having the best flowerbed in the neighborhood, rekindling a gardening interest I'd had since childhood. I enjoyed reading all kinds of inspirational and informative books, including the Bible. I enjoyed all these things and found them to be a refreshing break from work.

I WANTED TO MAKE A THIRTY YEAR CAREER OUT OF BASS FISHING. IF I HAD KEPT UP THE SAME INTENSITY... I WOULD HAVE BURNED OUT.

For me these intermittent escapes from bass fishing were a necessity to keep from burning myself out. I wanted to make a thirty year career out of bass fishing. If I had kept up the same intensity about bass fishing that I had in my early days, I would have

Fishing together on Sam Rayburn Lake in 1995 with my first team tournament partner, Steve Kastanes. In 1985, we finished fifth overall in the Oregon division of US Bass. Steve was a great partner who allowed me to grow, learn, and improve as a bass fisherman.

burned out. The chapter in my life when I lived the Skeeter Boats mantra of "eat, sleep, fish" was now closed, and life was marching on in a new direction.

Giving

In the last few years, I had become very involved in the Christian community. I was active at our home church with different prayer committees, men's Bible study groups, and church functions. I became an active leader at the Fellowship of Christian Anglers meetings at all the tournaments—the same meetings I had avoided years earlier. I also received many invitations for speaking engagements at churches and other Christian-related events around the country. I was available to God, and he was using me to share His gospel with fishermen all over America. The highs I experienced from serving others in Christian ministry were extremely satisfying. I was really getting into the idea of God using me to help others.

Right after my college graduation it was just me and the bass, and I could pursue bass fishing with singular devotion. However, it wasn't just me and the bass anymore. Now I had a wonderful wife, two amazing children, a half-dozen sponsors or more, speaking engagements across the country, tournaments to fish, a portfolio to manage, and ministry to do. Not to mention, I wanted to spend time with other family members and friends. I became one busy dude, but life was better than ever!

Prioritizing

One of the things I had to learn was how important it was to keep my priorities in order. When you keep your Biblical priorities in line, it leads to a balanced, fruitful life. Biblical priorities are centered on relationships: God comes first, wife second, children third, job fourth, and local church/ministry fifth. I have diligently worked to keep these priorities in order ever since I became a Christian, and it has paid off in many ways.

In 1998, Jill and I had two young girls, and our thoughts turned to their education and their childhood. At the time, we were enjoying our nice country home on the golf course at Rayburn Country in Sam Rayburn, Texas. We had lived at Rayburn for seven years now, but Rayburn Country is predominantly a retirement area with very few young children, and the area had limited schools and few cultural opportunities. The main attraction to Rayburn for us seven years ago had been the lake itself. However, we were entering a different chapter in our lives by raising a family, and it was time

IT WASN'T JUST ME AND THE BASS ANYMORE. ONE OF THE THINGS I HAD TO LEARN WAS HOW IMPORTANT IT WAS TO KEEP MY PRIORITIES IN ORDER.

Friend, Don Winebarger, (left) and Jerry Phelps, my neighbor and my spiritual mentor, (right) pose with the Classic trophy in my office at home in Tyler, Texas. All the sincere congratulations and support from the home crowd meant so much!

to move on to something else.

We thought about a city more centrally located for tournaments, possibly in Knoxville, Chattanooga, or Birmingham. We visited each city, looking at real estate and schools. Then, one day as I was driving from Rayburn up to the Skeeter factory in Kilgore, Texas, I heard the Holy Spirit whisper, "Go check out Tyler, Texas"—a nearby city of about 90,000 people in the rolling hills of East Texas. Jill and I did, and we fell in love with Tyler. Its biggest draws were its outstanding Christian schools, great churches, and many opportunities for kids.

As we began our search for a home in Tyler, I let Jill pick out the location of our new home. I would have loved to live on a lake or on another golf course, and we looked at some beautiful properties on both. However, I put my desires on the back burner. I traveled a lot, and I wanted to make sure my wife felt completely safe and secure when I was on the road. Jill and I picked out a nice home in a new subdivision, surrounded on two sides by deacons at our new church. Jill loved the place, and I have never regretted putting Jill's desires before mine.

Family

New Money

I had acquired more sponsors, including Yamaha, Lowrance, and Motorguide. I was now more valuable as a marketing entity to my sponsors, so they were all asking for more of my time. Companies asked for my input on projects like product development, field-testing, photo and video shoots, and outdoor writer workshops. I was also in greater demand as a speaker at fishing seminars. I made extra money doing seminars; however, they also took up more time in my increasingly busy schedule. The more successful I became, the more in demand I was as a public speaker.

I was also learning about money management. I was thirty-years old, but I had never had any money to save and invest before that time. I had always used every penny I made just to pay my bills. So having money was something new to me.

I HAD NEVER HAD ANY MONEY TO SAVE AND INVEST... I HAD ALWAYS USED EVERY PENNY I MADE JUST TO PAY MY BILLS. HAVING MONEY WAS SOMETHING NEW TO ME.

I knew nothing about the financial markets, so at first I gave my money to an investment professional. This strategy would have worked if he had made some decent returns for me. Unfortunately, he didn't. This was right at the start of the great bull market in the late '90s. Even index funds were doing a lot better than my guy. Being the competitor that I am, I finally came to the point where I couldn't take the underperformance anymore, and I pulled my money.

I was told it was the "new economy" where any kid with a PC could make money in the markets! So I tried my hand at investing. I did pretty well on my own at first during that great bull market, but then the internet bubble popped in March 2000, and I lost a bunch of cash.

Investing is just like any other sport, business, or competitive environment. There are quite a few people who know how to play the game and are decent at it, a whole lot fewer who are good at it, and just a handful who are really great at it. As a fisherman, I spend my time fishing, and that is my expertise. When weekend warriors come out and try to compete with me or other top pros, most of the time we take their money. It is just the same in the financial markets. If anyone who does something else for a living plays the financial markets against the pros, the pros are going to walk away with the money most of the time. I have learned that lesson the hard way.

MY FRIEND, ART FERGUSON, CALLED ME THAT NIGHT. HE TOLD ME I NEEDED TO ASK GOD FOR THE WIN AND HAVE FAITH TO BELIEVE IT WAS GOING TO HAPPEN.

Experience has shown me that the best way to invest money is to find someone who has a talent or gift for managing it. I say find someone with an excellent, proven track record over a period of at least five years and let them take care of it for you. It might cost you a little extra for a really good manager, but remember the old adage about how you get what you pay for.

Letting God In

During my maturing process, I was learning to incorporate prayer into all areas of my life, even in my tournaments! At the 2001 BASSMASTER Missouri Invitational at Table Rock Lake, I was in sixth place going into the final day of competition. My friend, Art Ferguson, called me that night. I heard an unfamiliar urgency in his voice. He told me that I needed to ask God for the win and have the faith to believe it was going to happen. Art encouraged me to pray for the win. I prayed, I believed, and the next day I won the tournament.

Believe it or not, that was the first time I can recall praying to win a fishing tournament. I'd always felt that praying that way was too self-centered. However, I frequently pray that the winner will give God the glory for the victory. That is the bottom line. It doesn't matter so much to me who the winner is, as long as he gives God the glory. I know I can't win all the time. The best bass fishermen of all time only win about 6 percent of the tournaments they fish. Even though that may have been the first time I prayed to win, I will say it won't be my last!

I have seen the positive effects of prayer in many situations. One time, an employee with one of my biggest sponsors wanted to make wholesale changes in the pro staff. The guy making this decision had some major personal problems, and he decided to stroke his ego and vent his frustrations by firing a few choice pro staff members who he envied. I caught wind of his schemes to can some of the veterans, including my dear friend Alton Jones, and myself. Instead of losing my temper or calling that guy on the carpet, I called Alton on the phone and asked him to pray with me. Jesus said, "Where two or three come together in my name, there am I with them," (Matthew 18:20). We prayed together that this injustice would not take place. Our prayers were intense. We finished our prayer and left it up to God to work out the problem. Would you believe that one week later that employee was fired?

I also began to understand God's spiritual law of reciprocity and became a generous giver. The Bible says that when you give, you will receive. As I matured as a Christian, I realized everything is really God's. When that revelation hit me, it became a whole lot easier to give. Then I started noticing the spiritual law of reciprocity at work. The more I gave, the more I received.

Our pastor at Green Acres Baptist Church in Tyler once challenged the congregation to give a special offering to the church, above and beyond our normal tithe to help pay off a new sanctuary we had just built. Jill and I went home and prayed about it, asking God how much we should give. We felt the Lord impressing on us to give $1,000 for each person in our family, so the next Sunday I wrote the church a check for $4,000. That is a lot of money for a fisherman!

I STARTED TO NOTICE THE SPIRITUAL LAW OF RECIPROCITY AT WORK. THE MORE I GAVE, THE MORE I RECEIVED.

Courage

Two days later, I left home for Tennessee to fish the BASS-MASTER Megabucks tournament. During the three-day practice period for Megabucks, I found some fish, but they were nothing special. The night before the competition began, I went to the partner pairings and got paired with an amateur, Buster Lily, who was a local expert on Douglas Lake. As we discussed our plans for the opening round of competition, it became clear that Buster was a very good fisherman who knew what he was talking about. He said he was onto some big ones up the river. I had never done this before in my thirteen year pro career, but the Holy Spirit was telling me to just forget about my fish and go with Buster to his spots up river. That is extremely hard to do on the first day of a major tournament! Maybe if it was the second or third day and I hadn't been doing well, following Buster would have been an easier choice to make.

I WAS LEARNING TO BE A MAN OF FAITH, AND MORE IMPORTANTLY, I WAS LEARNING TO RECOGNIZE WHEN GOD WAS PROMPTING ME TO DO SOMETHING.

But I was learning to be a man of faith, and more importantly, I was learning to recognize when God was prompting me to do something. I went with Buster right out of the gate on the opening round. We went to his spots upriver, and I caught fourteen pounds in less than an hour! I ended the day in second place with around 15 pounds of bass. I wound up fourth in that tournament and won $40,000—ten times as much as I had given to my church the week before! I have fished in over 160 BASSMASTER tournaments and never before has an amateur put me on any fish, let alone $40,000 worth of fish!

Giving

The key was to give cheerfully, expecting nothing in return. You can't broker a deal with God and say, "Lord, I am going to give this much to your church, and I am expecting this much in return." It doesn't work that way. I gave to my church willingly, never considering a return on my gift. My motives were pure. It felt good to give. Being able to give generously and then receiving God's blessing was even better.

Learning by Example

I've expressed how important it is to have mentors to help nurture and encourage us in our career responsibilities and various roles in our family and society. This is especially true in the area of spirituality. Just as Bill Sedar laid the foundation for my fishing career, I have had five men who have been spiritual mentors in my life. Passing down a living faith from generation to generation is extremely important to the health of the church and the Christian faith. Young Christians need to see living examples of Christianity in action.

As a young Christian, I knew what I was supposed to do on Sunday but wasn't quite so sure about the rest of the week. Applying Christian faith to my daily life was new territory for me, and I needed to see other men model faith in action. I learned to "walk the walk" during these seven years beside some of the most outstanding, godly men I've ever known. These five spiritual mentors have meant the world to me. With their help and guidance, I have matured into the man I am today. Some of their names are recognizable as part of the professional bass fishing world. Other names most people wouldn't know, but they are proof that any of us can have a life-changing impact on someone.

When I first was saved in 1993, I had one good Christian role model in my life. He was a fellow in Jasper, Texas named **Sparky Sparks.** I first met Sparky at Tanglewood Baptist Church in Jasper, Texas where Jill and I eventually attended. He and his wife, Mary, taught the Sunday school class for young married couples. We hit it off right away. Sparky loved to bass fish, and we started going together pretty regularly up to Sam Rayburn.

We became good friends and remain so to this day. Sparky heads up the Parole and Probation department of Jasper County. He is an honest and fair man, and he always tries to help the convicts by sharing the love of God with them. Sparky showed me that it is possible to take your faith into the workplace to try and help others.

Sparky leads by example. He is well respected in the community, very active in his church, and his family adores him. Sparky has also shown me how good it is to pray for others faithfully. Every time I would see him, even just in passing, he always told me he had been praying for Jill and me. I began to realize how far I needed to come with my prayer life.

When I moved to Tyler, Texas in 1998, I met one of my neighbors **Jerry Phelps** through a mutual friend. Jerry is the real deal. What you see is what you get. He pastors Tyler Metro Church, a non-denominational church in town. Early in my Christian walk I couldn't relate to any of the pastors I met. We didn't share any of the same interests. For my first five years as a Christian, I didn't meet a pastor that could be a role model for me–but then I met Jerry.

FOR MY FIRST FIVE YEARS AS A CHRISTIAN, I DIDN'T MEET A PASTOR THAT COULD BE A ROLE MODEL FOR ME—BUT THEN I MET JERRY. I SUSPECT JERRY LOVES TO FISH MORE THAN I DO.

No man has taught me more about what it is to be a Christian than Jerry. Although he preaches Christianity from the pulpit every Sunday morning, Jerry leads by example throughout the week. He exudes the love of Christ. Jerry and I jog together around the neighborhood, and we love to go fishing together. In fact, Jerry prefished with me before the 2002 BASSMASTERS Classic that I won. I suspect Jerry loves to fish more than I do. Jerry goes bass fishing every Friday, and he has done so for the last seventeen years. I am talking about every Friday, fifty-two weeks a year. It doesn't matter if it is pouring rain or blowing 60 mph. At sixty years of age, he can still wear me out in the boat. In fact, I don't even like to go with him anymore in the summer.

It will be 110 degrees out at 3:00 p.m. on a scorching hot July afternoon, and he will not come off the water. One time he was up at Lake Fork and the fish were biting so well that he just stayed all day and then all night! He fished for twenty-four hours straight!

Jerry and his wife Martha are an inspiration to Jill and me. Jerry prays for my family regularly, and he is always there if I have any spiritual questions.

Jim Phillips is another great friend I have made through fishing. Jim pastors North Greenwood Baptist Church in Greenwood, Mississippi. He also loves to bass fish, and he fishes quite a few tournaments at the semi-pro level. I got to know Jim through the various BASSMASTER tournaments he has competed in both as an amateur and a pro. Jim also serves as tournament director for the North Mississippi division of the Fishers of Men Tournament Trail. While still meeting his obligations as a full-time pastor of a church 1,200 members strong, Jim is following God's call to expand his ministry to the bass fishing world.

Jim always treats others with love and compassion. He is quite outspoken concerning his faith when he shares a boat with someone; however, he does it with a loving spirit. He is faithfully up at 4:00 a.m. every day, having his quiet time with the Lord and reading the Bible. He has prayed for me on a daily basis ever since I first met him. What a great friend! Jim has also been a great source for answers to my questions about the Bible. He knows it well and even teaches a Bible course to high school kids at private schools back in Mississippi.

I have another neighbor who is also a mentor for me—**Paul Conser.** Paul and I both attend Green Acres Baptist Church in Tyler, Texas. In addition to his deacon duties at Green Acres, Paul teaches Sunday School to third graders and serves on various committees at church. Paul is retired, so I see him nearly

I GOT TO KNOW JIM THROUGH THE VARIOUS **BASSMASTER** TOURNAMENTS HE HAS COMPETED IN BOTH AS AN AMATEUR AND A PRO.

every day when I am home. I have grown to have tremendous respect for this fine family man.

Paul is a stalwart when it comes to spiritual warfare and prayer, and he is the venerable prayer warrior of our neighborhood. Paul has prayed for me and my family daily ever since I met him about five years ago. He sure has raised the standard for my prayer life. I would love to one day leave the kind of legacy that Paul Conser will; he is the kind of man who has made America great.

DAVID IS A TRUE CHRISTIAN LEADER. HE HAS SHOWN ME THAT I CAN BE A CHRISTIAN AND STILL BE ONE OF THE BEST IN THE WORLD AT MY PROFESSION.

The current pastor at the church Paul and I attend is **Dr. David Dykes.** David is a true Christian leader. He has shown me that I can be a Christian and still be one of the best in the world at my profession. Watching a world-class performer in any profession is a soul-satisfying experience, and David's preaching on a Sunday morning is a beautiful thing. He is unbelievably good at using the art and science of motivational speaking in a professional manner. David successfully juggles the demands of being a husband and father, as well as being a pastor to 11,000 Texans. He is an author, teacher, world evangelist, mentor, music lover, and multi-engine rated pilot all the while finding the time every week to maintain his six handicap on the golf course. He is living proof that a personal relationship with Jesus can empower a man to do more than he ever dreamed possible.

Leading by Example

Like I've said before, it's important to have friendships with people who are at the same spiritual and emotional level you are. I am very appreciative of my friendships with my Christian brothers. Their strong faith has encouraged me, and their prayers have sustained me throughout these past few years. The Bible says, "As iron sharpens iron, so one man sharpens another,"

(Proverbs 27:17). My relationships with Alton Jones, Mark Davis, Art Ferguson, and David Gregg have meant a great deal to me in this respect. I also have friends to whom I have been a spiritual mentor of sorts, including pros Mike Auten and Kelly Jordon, as well as Jeff Barnes, a retired pro.

I thank God for the relationships I have with all of these great men of God. They have shown me how to live a successful Christian life in spite of trials. My relationships with these men **Mentoring** have been an integral part of my maturing in the Christian faith. It is one thing to read the Bible or a book on Christian living, but it's quite another to learn from someone's life. Until an immature Christian meets real people he can relate to and with whom he can share common interests, the Christian life never quite clicks. A large part of maturing in the Christian faith is simply following the lead of exemplary Christians. Their friendships, wisdom, and support were invaluable as I entered the most notable year of my career, 2002.

SECTION THREE:
SUCCESS

When the artist inside us uses
his or her own creative energies to
produce an original 'masterpiece',
we are at our best.

—An epiphany I had while
"in the zone"

Chapter Seven

THE ART OF BASS FISHING

Growing in wisdom and understanding and becoming a spiritually mature person are great blessings. However, you don't win World Championships simply by becoming spiritually mature. That is a big part of winning, but there is a lot more to it than that. If being spiritually mature were all there was to it, I imagine the evangelist Billy Graham could have won the Classic several times by now! Besides maturing as a person, I had also spent the last several years maturing into a champion angler.

I have been involved in professional bass fishing for the last fifteen years—a long time in professional sports. The media used to refer to me as a young, up-and-coming angler, but I don't hear that phrase anymore. Now they refer to me as a salty old veteran of the bass wars. And there are plenty of days where I really feel like one! The pro angler's lifestyle really takes it out of you.

After fifteen years, I feel like I am beginning to forget more than most people know about this sport! However, fishing is one sport where experience is an asset. In fact, having a veteran's view of the sport played a huge role in my win at the 2002 BASSMASTERS Classic World Championship. Wisdom and experience are two key elements in a competitive fisherman's makeup.

I don't consider myself a fast learner. I just accumulate fishing wisdom from experience. In the last fifteen years, I have fished for bass in nearly every state in the union, and I've caught them in each one, with the exception of only six or seven states. I have seen just about every imaginable type of lake or river in

When you're "in the zone," everything flows naturally, and there is tremendous calm.

America. The diversity of water in this country is amazing. Even more amazing, however, is the adaptability of bass—a fish that thrives in every state except Alaska.

Fishing is both an art and a science. Understanding the science of bass fishing is a prerequisite to success and involves matching the lures and techniques to the current conditions an angler faces. Anyone picking up the sport of fishing for the first time must learn the science first. My mentor, Bill Sedar, taught me the science of bass fishing and laid the foundation for my entire career. Unfortunately, most people spend their lives fishing at this level and never progress. In my opinion, the science of fishing is the rather mundane, albeit necessary, part of the sport.

My love for the sport centers on its intrinsic elements. As fishermen, once we master the fundamentals of the science of bass fishing, we are free to become creative artists. As artists, we exercise our creative liberties, bass rod in hand. God is extremely creative. Since He made us in His likeness, He wants us to use our creative talents as well, regardless of our field or occupation. When the artist inside us uses his or her own creative energies to produce an original "masterpiece," we are at our best.

Creativity Begins with Confidence

God has made us all uniquely different. Because of our individuality, no two people have the exact same fishing style. That's even more amazing when you consider the approximate number of sportsfishermen in the U.S. is around fifty million. People are all wired a little differently with different personalities. Besides that, our unique fishing experiences have helped mold us into the anglers we are today. No other fisherman has experienced what you have on the water. From the place you learned to fish, to your mentor or teacher, to all the conditions and lakes you have seen, no other fisherman has seen what you have seen. No wonder each fisherman is uniquely different.

That being the case, we hinder ourselves by limiting our creative genius when we try to go out for a day's fishing and fish like someone else. This sad scenario of playing the role of a fishing copycat keeps most anglers from ever reaching their full potential in the sport. Anytime anglers ask someone else for information on where the fish are biting or what they are biting on, they stifle their own creativity and limit their potential as anglers. I hear young guys on the Tour come along all the time

WE HINDER OURSELVES BY LIMITING OUR CREATIVE GENIUS WHEN WE TRY TO GO OUT FOR A DAY'S FISHING AND FISH LIKE SOMEONE ELSE.

and make the mistake of saying they want to have a fishing style like their favorite top pro. They don't last long on the Tour.

Here is where confidence comes into play. Confident fishermen aren't concerned about how anyone else does it or where anyone else is catching fish. They focus on getting into their own game, just being themselves on the water. That is when the original, creative, artistic talents begin to flow. This is exactly why the top pros like Kevin Van Dam, Rick Clunn, Denny Brauer, Mark Davis, and Gary Klien are so good. They believe in themselves; they know who they are as fishermen. Because they don't care about what other fishermen are doing, their streamlined creative genius flows without interruption. They are able to fish in the purest form and get the maximum out of their creative, artistic abilities.

THE TOP GUYS IN THE SPORT OF PROFESSIONAL BASS FISHING TODAY ARE ALL PURE ARTISTS. THEY ALWAYS HAVE CONFIDENCE IN THEIR OWN ABILITIES AND TALENTS.

The top guys in the sport of professional bass fishing today are all pure artists on the water. They always have confidence in their own abilities and talents and never fish anybody else's way but their own. I have a lot of respect for these guys as fishermen. When the top guys do well, you can count on the fact that their work is an original masterpiece.

In contrast, when anglers lack confidence in their own creative abilities and talents, they often go looking for help from others. This strategy always limits performance in the end. Relying too heavily on others puts a lid on what a fisherman can accomplish in this sport. It is similar to putting a governor on an engine to regulate its speed. Likewise, relying too heavily on others means an angler will only perform to a certain level. These anglers will never be free to utilize their creative abilities and become the fisherman God intended them to be.

Unfortunately, many fishermen become addicted to getting help from others. This addiction plagues our sport today, and it is such a shame. This destructive addiction starts out innocently enough. An angler gets a tip from someone else that pays off in a nice catch of fish. There is nothing intrinsically wrong with getting a tip and having it pay off. However, the problem comes when anglers begin to close their minds to their own original, creative thoughts and begin seeking advice from others as their main means to finding and catching fish.

At that point, the game is based on who can find the best advice. These anglers channel all their creative and artistic energies into seeing who can get the best help. Many fishermen have played this game for so long that they have totally forgotten who they are as fishermen. They have totally forgotten their unique individuality as an angler. They don't realize that without it, they are nobody special in terms of being an artist. They are just generic people replicating generic art, which contributes to the mire of mediocrity—perhaps the biggest tragedy of all. This is not the American dream. In the arts, reproductions are never quite as good as the original. Whether it's music, painting, or film, the original is always the best work. The same holds true in the art of fishing. Copycats never make it to the top.

WHETHER IT'S MUSIC, PAINTINGS, OR FILM, THE ORIGINAL IS ALWAYS THE BEST WORK. THE SAME HOLDS TRUE IN THE ART OF FISHING. COPYCATS NEVER MAKE IT TO THE TOP.

I have always seen the value of doing original, creative work in my fishing. Ever since I started fishing professionally, I have tried to follow this creed. Even as I worked out my own creativity early in my career, I had mixed results. I still made plenty of mistakes. One of my most common mistakes was trying to force things to happen out on the water. My mindset was, "I am going to do this my way and force the fish to eat this lure." However, I always bombed with that strategy. Another one of my big mistakes has been trying to go for the home run too often. This is similar to swinging too hard on the golf course. I would do something that, in my intellect, made sense for a big stringer, but that was all it was, my intellect. I would always fail miserably. I have learned that my mind can't figure out the fish; I'm just not wise enough.

My lifelong lesson has been to learn through trial and error that I can't accomplish everything I want on my own. All of my successes have stemmed from following the Holy Spirit (not other fishermen or my own intellect) and just doing what felt right. I like to call it "fishing by feel." I learned a long time ago that God loves it when I give Him a chance to lead me in my fishing. If I go to other fishermen looking for advice or if I am bullheaded and try to swing for the fences or force my way on the fish, I am not giving God a chance to lead me or guide me. However, when I pray for advice and listen to the still, small voice of the Holy Spirit, there is no end to what God can do through me. That's true concerning every area of our lives, fishing included. I explain more about the Holy Spirit in the Afterword section at the end of this book.

> **PEACE IS A HUGE COMMON DENOMINATOR IN WORLD CLASS FISHING PERFORMANCES. SOME CALL IT BEING "IN THE ZONE."**

Peace and Rhythm

All fishermen know how it feels when things don't go well on the water. As pro fishermen, when things are not working and we aren't catching fish during competition, this feeling of frustration multiplies. When we look at our watch and see time slipping away as the fishing day draws to a close, panic often sets in. What a terrible emotion. When panic sets in, it ruins your day every time. In contrast, peace is God's signature style; it's how He does everything.

Peace is a huge common denominator in world class fishing performances. Some call it being "in the zone." All I know is that you enter this special place where everything flows naturally, it all seems so easy, and there is tremendous calm. Fishing is no longer a struggle; you are not fighting anything (except big green fish). It is like you are on cruise control and God is taking care of your day, making things happen. It is almost like walking right into something predetermined. I've experienced a few of those wonderful days, most recently during my win at the 2002 BASS-MASTERS Classic, but not nearly enough of them!

Do your very best not to let distractions get the best of you and rob you of your peace. If someone offends you on the water and your emotions flare, it's all over. This is one reason why Focus most of the top fishing talents seek out isolated fishing areas away from the crowds. They realize they can perform better when they can keep their emotions in check. Fishing is the opposite of a sport like football, where emotions are a big asset. When it comes to having the proper mindset for competition, fishing is more like golf where a little emotion is good—but just a little.

DO YOUR BEST TO NOT LET DISTRACTIONS GET THE BEST OF YOU AND ROB YOU OF YOUR PEACE. IF SOMEONE OFFENDS YOU ON THE WATER AND YOUR EMOTIONS FLARE, IT'S ALL OVER.

Rhythm is also a huge component of successful fishing, as it is in golf, one of my favorite sports. I definitely find the peace of God alongside a good rhythm on the water. The top pros find a bait that is working, and they stick with it. In virtually all of my wins and most of my top finishes, I found a lure and technique that were working, and I just stayed with them. That strategy builds rhythm. Jumping back and forth between lures and techniques ruins rhythm and is a detriment to fishing success.

At times, rhythm requires tremendous discipline, especially when you are aware of other patterns that are working. Establishing a rhythm with a certain lure lets you fully capitalize on its potential. If the quality fish prefer the lure you are establishing your rhythm with, you can win. Shallow water fishermen benefit especially well from establishing a rhythm as it is a big asset to casting accuracy. An accurate caster will catch more fish. It is very hard to cast accurately when switching back and forth between different lures weighing varying amounts.

Mindset of a Winner

The art of fishing entails other variables besides originality, creativity, peace, and rhythm. The proper mindset is also necessary to success. Early in my career, I was extremely hungry for success in professional bass fishing. I worked hard and pressed in with all my might to see my dream become reality. By the time I won the Superstars in 1995, I had realized my dream. I wasn't the top bass pro in the land, but I was close. I had bought a nice home, I had some major sponsorships, and I had found the success I was looking for in my tournaments. I had arrived as a top player. I wasn't *the* top player, mind you, but I was one of the top ten in the world.

INSTANTLY, I FOUND MYSELF DEALING WITH SOMETHING NEW IN MY LIFE I HAD NEVER EXPERIENCED BEFORE. I ENTERED A COMFORT ZONE. I HAD NEVER THOUGHT ABOUT WHAT I'D DO AFTER I BECAME SUCCESSFUL.

Instantly, I found myself dealing with something new in my life I had never experienced before. I entered a comfort zone. I had spent my whole life up until that point toiling to achieve my dream. Then one morning I woke up, and I had arrived. I was there. I was the fisherman I had always dreamed of becoming. I was unprepared for that realization. I had never thought about what I'd do after I became successful; I was always too concerned with becoming successful in the first place. Now I needed to start learning how to deal with my success.

When I hit this comfort zone, something inside me changed. I still went through the motions, but the passion was missing. My heart just was not in it like it used to be. In a comfort zone, your human nature kicks in and wants to sit back, relax, and enjoy the victor's spoils. You see, working your way to the top (or very close to the top) of a profession takes an incredible amount of hard work. Very little of it is fun. Being driven to succeed means you pay the price physically, emotionally, and relationally. You certainly don't enjoy the easy life this American culture tells you winners deserve.

Over the next couple of years, I had to work through this comfort zone stage in my fishing. Thankfully, I still performed well enough to fish in the Classic each summer. The dangerous part about being in a comfort zone is that you can recognize it, tell yourself you'll deal with it, and yet never really leave it. Let's face it: comfort zones are a pleasant place to be. The problem for a professional bass fisherman is that if he stays in a comfort zone for long, he will no longer have a job. The environment is just too competitive.

Fortunately, I realized despite their appearance to the contrary, comfort zones don't let us live life at its best. The best life Focus

has to offer comes when we are pressing toward a goal or purpose. God was calling me to forget my past successes and press on! Pressing on is part of life, plain and simple. It involves lots of work and little rest. We can never reach another level of performance if we are in a comfort zone. If anything, that comfort zone might set us back a couple of levels. One day, I discovered the truth about pressing on when I read Philippians 3:13-14 about ". . . forgetting those things which are behind and reaching forward to those things which are ahead, I press towards the goal for the prize of the upward call of God in Christ Jesus," (NKJV).

Pride in our past accomplishments does nothing to ensure future success. Good or bad, our past does not matter. Only the future counts, not what we did or did not accomplish yesterday. This mindset keeps us from resting on our past success and helps us maintain a strong work ethic. Mentally, that is right where we need to be.

PRIDE IN OUR PAST ACCOMPLISHMENTS DOES NOTHING TO ENSURE FUTURE SUCCESS. GOOD OR BAD, OUR PAST DOES NOT MATTER.

The remaining variables that sometimes shape our day of

fishing are often beyond our control. I am referring to what some call "luck." Yes, pure chance does play a role in fishing just as it does in life. The Bible says in Ecclesiastes 9:11, "time and chance happen to all men." We have all been recipients of both good and bad "luck." Fish are lost, outboard motors break, and we stumble upon the mother lode of bass. However, we can't get emotionally involved with experiences related to "time and chance." **We can't control when our "time" comes or when "by chance" something happens to us on the water. Focus your attention on those factors over which you do have control** and leave the rest to God. When time and chance don't go my way, I just rest in the promise that has become my life verse, "And we know that all things work together for good to those who love God, to those who are the called according to His purpose," (Romans 8:28).

Work Ethic

Success starts with a passion in your heart for what you are doing. You must also be driven to work extremely hard and go the extra mile to see your plans succeed. Being driven always involves living on the "uncomfortable edge," which sets you apart from the crowd. The best never rest, and they certainly don't enjoy a soft, comfortable life.

In any business or sport, when you possess the passion and the drive, you must next come up with your own way of being creative. This is an absolute necessity if you want to reach the top of your profession. Being an original, creative artist in your field takes time. I have learned that you can't rush creativity. You certainly can't rush God, the author of original creativity.

Being at peace with your personal life and with your daily schedule is also critical. Where there's no peace, there's no rhythm. And finally, my relationship with God must come above all else. God holds the key to unlocking all the potential within me.

Relaxed...frustrated...disgusted...thrilled!

—Just a few of my feelings during the FLW tournament.

Chapter Eight

THE VIEW FROM THE TOP

■t's easy for a pro to beat guys who only fish for a hobby. Those who fish on the semi-pro level put up a bit of a struggle, but they are no match for a touring professional. When I hit the pro tour, the competition grew a whole lot tougher for me. These guys were good. With a little help from above, I got to where I could beat most touring pros regularly. But those last six or seven superstars at the top of the profession? I could never quite catch them, at least not until 2002.

Viewing my career from the summit of my profession, I would have to say that the final leap to the top, beating those last six or seven guys, was the hardest new level to reach. I didn't have much trouble rising to the top back in my younger days in Oregon. Achieving success at the next level, in the premier Western Trails, was a bit tougher. Then things really started getting difficult when I tried my hand at being one of the top pros in the nation. However, reaching the top spot in my profession? That took me fifteen years.

It's All in the Timing

I fished both professional tournament trails in 2002: the BASSMASTER Tour and the FLW Tour. My regular season on the BASSMASTER Tour was not very exciting. Other than a ninth place finish on the Red River, I only made the money (top forty) one other time out of six tournaments. I finished the regular season in thirtieth place overall, just barely qualifying for the 2002 Classic.

On the other hand, I could do no wrong on the FLW Tour, where I won my first national AOY title in 2002. In the past, I have only been able to speculate about what it takes to win a national AOY title. Now that I have lived through one, I have found the keys to winning simply astounding. The keys to winning a national title are not what I ever thought they would be.

THE KEYS TO WINNING A NATIONAL TITLE ARE NOT WHAT I EVER THOUGHT THEY WOULD BE. SOMETIMES THE THINGS GOD TELLS US TO DO ARE NOT EASY, BUT WE STILL NEED TO OBEY.

For the previous four years, I did not participate in the FLW Tour events because none of the companies I worked with (Skeeter, Yamaha, Berkley, Daiwa, Lowrance, or Motorguide) sponsored the FLW Tour at that time. The FLW is a fine, professionally run tour, but their "no conflicting logos" policy in 1998 prevented me from wearing my sponsors' logos unless they also sponsored the FLW. I had fished in some of their events back in 1997 prior to this clothing policy. However, when they changed their rules, I felt I needed to be loyal to my sponsors and fish the tournaments that allowed me to promote them.

I prayed long and hard about this difficult decision. FLW was offering the best purses in the sport. However, God showed me that I was already making a good living, and I did not need to be greedy. Sometimes the things God tells us to do are not easy, but we still need to obey. It was tough seeing my peers win hundreds of thousands of dollars on the FLW Tour while I wasn't fishing. Even so, God gave me a peace I was doing the right thing for me.

In 2001, Yamaha and Berkley, two of my three biggest sponsors, became sponsors of the FLW Tour. In the summer that year, Phil Dyskow, the president of Yamaha Motor Corporation, asked me over lunch one day to fish the FLW Tour the coming year. Berkley thought it would also be a good idea. A third sponsor, Lowrance, also joined the FLW Tour as a sponsor with their Eagle brand of electronics. Now that my sponsors were behind me, I prayed about it and felt a release to go ahead and fish the tour in 2002.

I vividly remember confiding in my good friend Mike Auten, who had been abstaining from FLW for the same reasons as I did. I told him it wouldn't surprise me to see the Lord really bless us on the FLW Tour in 2002 since we had resisted the urge to compete for the big money. In fact, when I committed to fishing the FLW Tour in 2002, I heard that still, small voice of the Holy Spirit tell me, "You will now be blessed for your obedience." It was as plain as day.

I FELT VERY RELAXED AND LOOSE FROM THE START OF THE 2002 FLW SEASON. I HAD NEVER BEFORE ENTERED A SEASON WITH SUCH A RELAXED ATTITUDE.

I felt very relaxed and loose from the start of the 2002 FLW season. I had never before entered a season with such a relaxed attitude. To be honest, I initially fished the Tour because my sponsors wanted me to be there, not because I necessarily wanted to be there. The whole thing was just no big deal to me. At the beginning of the season, I was uncharacteristically carefree about my performance on the FLW Tour, almost apathetic.

Not only did I have a unique mindset going into the first tournament in January on the 2002 FLW Tour in south Florida at Lake Okeechobee, this tournament would also mark a milestone in my spiritual journey. All of these events worked together to set the stage for why I won top honors in 2002.

Building Momentum

My good friend and fellow Christian, Art Ferguson, was spending the winter at Okeechobee working as a guide at Roland Martins Marina in Clewiston. When I arrived in Clewiston for the FLW tournament, Art informed me his church, New Harvest, was having a revival that week, and he invited me to attend. There was definitely a time in my career, even as a Christian, when I would have never stayed up late each night during a tournament attending anything that might distract me from my fishing. However, after the first night at the revival, I couldn't wait to return each night. I was more excited about experiencing God at that revival than I was about the FLW tournament!

The evangelist, Tony Miller, made a special effort at the revival to encourage the young pastors who served in mission churches started by the Clewiston church. These young pastors were working so diligently for the Lord. One night, during the praise and worship, I made a covenant with God by praying this promise, "God, I love you so much that if I win the tournament this week, I will tithe the whole winner's purse of $100,000 to these young pastors and their churches." I had never done anything like that before. That was a lot of money to me, but I didn't care; I wanted to bless God.

I hadn't been on Okeechobee in eleven years, and I wasn't necessarily expecting a great finish in that tournament. I surprised myself and got on some really good sight fishing that week, spotting some big fish in shallow water. As the tournament progressed, I started moving up the leader board. I was getting really excited. Going into the final day, I found myself having a great shot at winning the tournament. I didn't know what God's plans were, but I was half expecting to win so that God would let me contribute that $100,000 into the work of those young pastors. I told Art about my covenant with the Lord for accountability's sake in case I ended up winning the thing. I also asked Art to share it with the Clewiston church so they would be praying for me. On the final day, some members of the church staff, including the pastor and his youth director, showed up to watch the weigh-in.

As I headed out to compete on the final day, I experienced

I WAS HALF EXPECTING TO WIN SO THAT GOD WOULD LET ME CONTRIBUTE THAT $100,000. I QUICKLY LEARNED THAT GOD DOESN'T NEED MY MONEY.

some new emotions. Personally, I had nothing to gain if I won. I had never been in that situation before, and it totally relieved me of any pressure. I had always experienced pressure while fishing for big money on the final day of a tournament. However, that day was so different. I wasn't nervous; my job was simply to go out that day and put forth a good effort for the Lord. I left the results up Him. I figured He was the one who stood to gain or lose that day, not me.

I quickly learned that God doesn't need my money. I wound up finishing third in that tournament, yet I learned a great lesson that week that paid off handsomely later in the year. As it turns out, I believe this lesson wasn't about money. It was about God trying to teach me the proper mindset for competition that week. When a competitor is loose and relaxed like I was, he performs at his or her best. Our job is to put forth a good day's work, not worry about the results, and instead leave them up to Him.

IT WAS ABOUT GOD TRYING TO TEACH ME THE PROPER MINDSET. OUR JOB IS TO PUT FORTH A GOOD DAY'S WORK, NOT WORRY ABOUT THE RESULTS, AND INSTEAD LEAVE THEM UP TO HIM.

Still, I was somewhat amazed I didn't win that event. As I reflected on my finish during the long drive home, I realized God had used my promise as a test. He wanted to see how faithful I would be to Him. By telling God I would give Him the purse if I won, I was not trying to broker a deal with Him. I was not trying to manipulate Him into blessing me. I made that promise out of my pure love for Him, not expecting anything in return. My heart was sincere; my motives were right. As it turns out, placing third allowed me to take home more money than I would have if I had won! My promise to God was to give all of my winnings to the church if I won the $100,000 first prize. Instead, I placed third and God gave me peace about taking home the $22,000 prize. God honored my willingness to be faithful to him. I believe I reached a milestone in my faith and Christian servanthood that

Patience

week in January 2002—a crucial prerequisite for reaching the next level professionally. I knew I was ready for whatever would come next.

Breaking All the Rules

That same carefree attitude and spiritual awareness carried over to the next FLW tournament at Lake Wheeler, Alabama in February. I went out the first day of practice and tried to catch them on power baits like jigs, spinnerbaits and crankbaits, and I had no success. Even though I knew the tournament would be won on one of those power baits, the water was 45 degrees in mid-winter in north Alabama, and I didn't feel like force-feeding power baits to the bass. So I put those power baits, along with my chances to win, away in my tackle box. Instead, I whipped out a 4-inch Berkley Finesse Worm, 8-pound line and a spinning rod—a rig notorious for small fish. I started getting bites right away. I began having so much fun staying bit that I never put down my spinning rod and little Power Worm. I finished twenty-eighth out of 175 fishermen that week.

I BELIEVE THE FACT THAT I WAS SO RELAXED AND CARE-FREE IN THE 2002 FLW TOUR ALLOWED ME TO FISH AT MY BEST.

A guy with a spinning rod fishing for small bass is not a likely candidate to win a national AOY title, mind you. All the pros know you need to fish for big fish to win that title. In fact, no one had ever won a national AOY title fishing with a finesse worm and a spinning rod. I was breaking all the rules, but I didn't care. This laissez-fare attitude was unusual for me. Winning AOY had always been my goal at the beginning of each BASSMASTER season, and I pushed for it, fishing in a manner I thought necessary to win that title. In contrast, I believe the fact that I was so relaxed and carefree in the 2002 FLW Tour allowed me to fish at my best.

An ironic twist began to occur. I was putting most of my effort into the BASSMASTER Tour in 2002. On the other hand, I would just show up at the FLW events and pretty much go through the motions. I would prefish as many of the BASSMASTER tournaments as I could, really putting some time in preparing for them. Yet I wasn't doing so well on the BASSMASTER Tour, and I was excelling on the FLW Tour. Conventional wisdom told me the exact opposite should have been taking place.

The third tournament on the 2002 FLW Tour was at Lake Ouachita, near Hot Springs, Arkansas. It was still cold in mid-March, and the fishing was terrible. The bass in Lake Ouachita had experienced a bout with the Largemouth Bass Virus in 2001, and many of the bass had died. On the first couple of practice days, I again tried to catch the quality bass needed to win on jigs, crankbaits and spinnerbaits. It was so cold that the bass were not responding well to these power baits—the same scenario I had seen at the last tournament at Lake Wheeler. Once again, I put the big fish lures, and my chance to win, away in my tackle box and pulled out my spinning rod and Berkley finesse worm. If I were pressing to win the AOY title, I would have tried to force the bass to eat a power bait in an attempt to catch bigger fish. But I wasn't pressing; I was as loose as a goose. Spinning rod in hand, I found some fish right away, drop-shotting the little worm in about 30 feet of water. I stuck with the drop-shot rig and ended up thirty-fourth in that tournament.

Since winning AOY on the FLW Tour still had not crossed my mind, I wasn't trying to force feed power baits to those bass at Wheeler and Ouachita where the fishing was so tough. Yet, when you go with a finesse worm during a tournament in the South, you immediately eliminate your chance to win. Even so, I felt no pressure to take charge and make things happen. I simply read the mood of the fish and figured out a way to catch them. I

WHEN YOU GO WITH A FINESSE WORM DURING A TOURNAMENT IN THE SOUTH, YOU IMMEDIATELY ELIMINATE YOUR CHANCE TO WIN.

155

didn't let reason get in the way. Our intellect can really mess us up sometimes. We try to force what we think is right or force our favorite technique on the fish. Sometimes we try too hard.

After Lake Ouachita, I was in third place in the AOY race. That was the first time I began to entertain the thought that I could possibly win the title. This realization triggered a change in my attitude. I didn't show up at any more FLW tournaments with the same carefree attitude. I began to press and work very hard in an attempt to reach what was now a very realistic goal.

In the Running

The fourth FLW event was in April at Beaver Lake, Arkansas. The fish were spawning, as they usually do in mid-April on Beaver Lake. I sight-fished the whole event and came away with a sixteenth place finish. I moved up a slot to second place in the AOY race. Sight-fishing, without casting until I visually spot a bass, has become one of my favorite techniques. When the bass are spawning, it is one of the best ways to catch a quality stringer. In the spring, it ranks right up there with jigs, crankbaits, and spinnerbaits as a proven big fish tournament-winning technique. And it soon came in handy in this AOY race.

OUR INTELLECT CAN REALLY MESS US UP SOMETIMES. WE TRY TO FORCE WHAT WE THINK IS RIGHT OR FORCE OUR FAVORITE TECHNIQUE ON THE FISH.

It became clear after the Beaver Lake tournament that only three men had a legitimate shot at AOY. At each FLW event, the winner gets 200 points, second place receives 199 points, and so on. Whoever has the greatest cumulative total at the end of the year wins the AOY title. Tour rookie Sam Newby was leading the points race. I was second, and the 2001 World Champion and Angler of the Year, Kevin Van Dam, was third. Everyone else was way behind.

I bore down on the fifth event, held on Old Hickory Lake in

Focus

Tennessee in May. The weather was warming, and my competitive juices were flowing. My attitude had done a complete 180-degree turn from the first half of the season. I had shifted into animal-mode, ready for the kill. I arose at four in the morning each day of practice and was on the water by five, while it was still dark outside. Early one morning at 5:00 a.m., a tremendous thunder and lightning storm passed through when I was on the water. I hardly noticed the torrential downpour and lightning popping all around me. I was pressing very, very hard. Everything in me wanted to beat Van Dam and win the AOY title.

Old Hickory ended up being the strangest tournament. I had an outstanding practice and felt as if I had located the fish to win the tournament, which does not happen often. I was catching them fishing a spinnerbait around boat docks. The bite was an early one, and the good spinnerbait fishing was over by 8:00 a.m. each day. It gets light at 5:30 a.m. in Tennessee in late May, though, so I figured I would have two and a half hours to work my pattern each morning.

I HAD SHIFTED INTO ANIMAL-MODE, READY FOR THE KILL.

I HARDLY NOTICED THE TORRENTIAL DOWNPOUR AND LIGHTNING POPPING ALL AROUND ME.

At the tournament briefing on the evening prior to the first day of competition, the tournament director announced that take-off each morning would be at 7:00 a.m. I sat up in my chair. "What?!" I said to myself. "Take-off one and a half hours after sunrise?" That was ludicrous. I had fished tournaments for fifteen years and had never heard of such a late start to a tournament day. Take-off is always at first safe light, usually right around sunrise.

This unexpected blow was really going to hurt my chances to do well in this crucial tournament. Instead of two and a half hours to fish my spinnerbait pattern, I would only have one hour between 7:00 and 8:00 a.m. I was devastated. (As it turned out, after talking to the tournament director later, he didn't mean to have such a late start. He had been posting take-off at all the other tournaments that year at 7:00 a.m., and he never thought about changing it to an earlier time due to the longer days of May). It was a simple, unintended oversight, but it was killing me.

The first day was sunny, and by the time I got on the water, the spinnerbait bite was over. I caught four bass the first day and was in about fiftieth place. The second day, the sky got cloudy, stretching out that crucial spinnerbait bite. I was paired that second day with an amateur named Danny Strand, an old friend I had previously fished with a couple of times. We started out with the spinnerbait pattern, and the bass were eating it much better due to the cloud cover.

I started catching them, but Danny started catching them better. I was moving fairly fast, wanting to cover as much water as I could before the spinnerbait bite was over. He was fishing from the back of the boat behind me, throwing his spinnerbait in the same boat slips I had just fished. Danny had caught a few small keepers, but then he caught a four-pounder, and I really started to get frustrated. I had just thrown my identical spinnerbait in that same boat slip twice, and that four-pound bass never touched my lure! Then Danny caught another big one out from behind another spot where I had just unsuccessfully thrown my lure! I could not figure out what I was doing wrong, and my frustration level intensified. Danny and I were fishing the exact same spinnerbait. I was making at least two casts to each boat slip with my spinnerbait. Yet when I finished fishing a slip, Danny would throw his identical spinnerbait in it and pull out a big bass. It was the darndest thing I had ever witnessed.

I had so much on the line, and I could not catch the fish. I had found the right spot, I had the right lure, and I couldn't catch them. I would pull up to a boat dock with a bass underneath it ready to eat the spinnerbait I had tied on. I would throw my spinnerbait under the dock, and

I COULD NOT FIGURE OUT WHAT I WAS DOING WRONG, AND MY FRUSTRATION LEVEL INTENSIFIED. IT WAS THE DARNDEST THING I HAD EVER WITNESSED.

I could not catch the fish. That is what you call having a bad day. Meanwhile, the amateur in the back of my boat would then throw the same lure to the same spot and easily catch the fish.

I slowed down and made even more casts to each spot before Danny did, but it didn't matter. He would still throw in behind me and pull out a big one! He finally caught his kicker fish, about a 6 1/2-pounder, and I was crushed. Don't get me wrong, I was happy for Danny that he was having such a good day. Inside, however, I was absolutely disgusted with myself because I was getting the first shot at all these fish and I could not catch them. The pressure riding on this tournament only made matters worse.

I WAS HAPPY FOR DANNY THAT HE WAS HAVING SUCH A GOOD DAY. INSIDE, HOWEVER, I WAS ABSOLUTELY DISGUSTED WITH MYSELF.

Danny ended the day with a five fish limit that weighed 16 pounds—his best day ever in ten years of fishing tournaments as an amateur. To put his phenomenal catch in perspective, the second best amateur stringer that day was only 8 pounds. Danny's catch doubled the next best amateur stinger—an unheard of feat. If that weren't enough, his limit was also bigger than any pro limit that day. An amateur had never waxed me so badly in my fifteen years of tournament fishing. What a terrible time for that to happen, too, with AOY up for grabs.

I caught four bass weighing 8 pounds that day and ended up thirty-sixth in the tournament. Meanwhile, Kevin Van Dam finished third at Old Hickory, and he took a commanding lead in the AOY race. Sam Newby bombed out and fell way back in the pack. I remained in second place in the AOY race, a distant 28 points behind Van Dam. The AOY race was over as far as I was concerned. After my career-worst performance at Old Hickory, I figured winning AOY wasn't meant to be. It just wasn't in the cards for me. Besides, Van Dam, the reigning BASSMASTERS Classic World Champ and 2001 FLW Angler of the Year, was now leading the race by a huge margin.

As I left the lake that day, I was depressed—big time. I was at a major low point of my career. This, in fact, was probably my worst tournament ever. I had placed much lower than thirty-sixth before, but this time I was finally contending for a national AOY title. I had located the very fish I needed to do really well in the event. I had even found the right lure to catch them on, but I couldn't catch them. My hands were tied. What was keeping me from catching those fish? It was a living nightmare!

Patience

I firmly believe that while most of the time God leaves the fishing up to us, there are definitely times when He makes the fish bite, and there are times when He keeps the fish from biting our hooks as well. I don't know how else to interpret what happened to me in that tournament. However, I kept reminding myself about Romans 8:28, knowing that God would use all these things to work for my good.

Breaking My Pride

I did some deep soul-searching after the Old Hickory tournament. I prayed for God to show me the error of my ways. I always want to learn from my mistakes and bad tournaments and become a better man as a result. You see, I had come a long way in my Christian maturity, but I was still not where God wanted me to be. After nine years of being a Christian, I still had some deep-rooted seeds of pride within my heart. These had to go before He could take me to the next level. The Bible declares in James 4:6, "God opposes the proud, but gives grace to the humble." One name kept coming up repeatedly during my prayers: Kevin Van Dam. He is a great guy, and he has done a wonderful job promoting the sport of bass fishing. However, he had created a problem for me.

AFTER NINE YEARS OF BEING A CHRISTIAN, I STILL HAD SOME DEEP-ROOTED SEEDS OF PRIDE WITHIN MY HEART.

God began to show me that I had a major issue of pride concerning Van Dam that I needed to resolve. It went back to the very beginning of my career. Van Dam and I are the same age, and we began our careers at the same time. Right away, people began comparing the two of us, saying we would be the next superstars in the sport of bass fishing. Which of us would be the greatest was a constant debate. BASS Times even conducted a poll of all of our peers back in 1990 to get the pros opinions on different subjects. One of the questions was, "Who is the best up-and-coming young pro?" Van Dam and I split the vote. There may have been a hanging chad in there somewhere, but it didn't matter. We were still neck and neck.

For the last twelve years, I have dealt with a huge amount of pride over constantly competing with Van Dam. He has stayed a step or two ahead of me our whole careers. At the end of 2001, he had won four national AOY titles and one World Championship. I had won none of the above. He had won seven B.A.S.S. tournaments to my four. He had bested me in every possible statistical category. Over the last twelve years, he had risen to fifth place on the B.A.S.S. all-time money list, and I was two steps behind in seventh place. Even though I had produced a stellar track record on the pro Tours over the last twelve years, it seemed like I was always fishing in his shadow.

WHICH OF US WOULD BE THE GREATEST WAS A CONSTANT DEBATE. VAN DAM AND I SPLIT THE VOTE. THERE MAY HAVE BEEN A HANGING CHAD IN THERE SOMEWHERE, BUT IT DIDN'T MATTER. WE WERE STILL NECK AND NECK.

It reminds me of what takes place on the PGA Tour with Tiger Woods and Phil Mickelson. Phil Mickelson is an extremely talented golfer, one of the best of his generation. Unfortunately, Phil happened to start his career at the same time as Tiger. Tiger Woods has turned into arguably the best golfer of all time, and Phil has played in Tiger's shadow his whole career. He has never been quite able to beat Tiger, especially in the majors. Kevin Van Dam is professional bass fishing's version of Tiger

Woods, and I can definitely relate to Phil.

I burned with envy every time Van Dam would beat me, and I would gloat with pride the few times I would beat him. I figured the AOY race would usher in my opportunity to finally beat Van Dam for a major title in bass fishing. I even had a lead on him going into the Old Hickory tournament. I was in second, and he was in third. Then my worst nightmare occurred. Van Dam finished third at Old Hickory, blowing right by me in the standings.

He had beaten me so many times, and I was so depressed after my lousy tournament at Old Hickory that I just threw in the towel. I totally gave up on my chances of winning the title. The pain was so great after Old Hickory that I didn't want to set myself up again for another bruising at the last tournament of the season on Lake Champlain, about three weeks away in New York. I had grown weary of hoping I could beat Van Dam.

Before I traveled up to New York for the season finale, I flew down to Disney World in Florida to compete in the Citgo Celebrity Challenge, a fishing tournament on the Disney lakes. Six bass pros and six NASCAR drivers paired up as teams. The bass pros included Van Dam, myself, Shaw Grigsby, Marty Stone, Gerald Swindle, and Earl Bentz. I fished with driver Kurt Busch and we had a good time at this one-day tournament with nothing much on the line. Kurt and I had a good catch that day, and I thought we might be able to win as we headed to the weigh-in. But no! We finished second. That cotton pickin' Van Dam had beat me again!

WHAT WAS MEANT TO BE A FUN, MADE-FOR-TV EVENT AT DISNEY WORLD BECAME THE STRAW THAT BROKE THE CAMEL'S BACK. IN MY HEART, MY PRIDE SNAPPED.

What was meant to be a fun, made-for-TV event at Disney World became the straw that broke the camel's back. In my heart, my pride snapped. Van Dam had totally, once-and-for-all crushed my competitive soul. Our competition was over. He had won. For the first time ever, I began to freely admit to anyone who would listen that Kevin Van

Dam was the best fisherman in the world. All my pride instantly vanished into the sultry summer air in Orlando. At the time, I had no idea what a victory this was in my walk with the Lord. I just felt like such a miserable failure.

As it turned out, my life was changed by my decision to let go of my pride and freely admit to everyone that Kevin Van Dam was better than me. Who would have ever guessed that the key to finally beating Van Dam rested in my ability to surrender my pride and admit he was the better fisherman? What a huge revelation! That was the key decision God had been waiting for me to make. It was a defining moment. In my next two tournaments, I instantly ramped to the next level in my fishing. God could now entrust fame and fortune to me. When I humbled myself, he willingly gave me grace after resisting my pride all those years.

MY LIFE WAS CHANGED BY MY DECISION TO LET GO OF MY PRIDE AND FREELY ADMIT TO EVERYONE THAT KEVIN VAN DAM WAS BETTER THAN ME.

Before that final FLW event of the season, I still had not grasped the full impact of releasing my pride even as my family and I made the drive up to New York. I had no way of knowing what God was about to do in my life after my defining moment in Orlando. At the time, I just felt like a little whipping boy for Kevin Van Dam. God used Van Dam to humble me to the extreme. I was, in fact, simply amazed at how good Van Dam really is. He is the best bass fisherman in the world today. Period.

The Final FLW Tournament

At that time, I was still in second place for the FLW AOY title, but I was 28 points behind Van Dam. Mentally, I had already conceded the race to him. I had that much respect for him as a fisherman. I fully realized that Van Dam's career record showed every time he had led a tournament or an AOY race going into the final day or the final tournament, he had always won. Always.

He is a very strong finisher, the mark of all true champions. In my mind, I had lost the AOY race the month before at Old Hickory when I bombed.

So much for the power of positive thinking, or in this case, the power of negative thinking. I came into that final FLW tournament fully convinced I was going to lose to Van Dam, and I won! Go figure that one out all you "visualization specialists!" I believe when God decides something is going to happen, no positive or negative visualization is going to change His will. When God decides it's your time to win, you win. Period.

On our drive up to Lake Champlain, I remember poking my head out from behind my veil of depression, admitting to Jill one glimmer of hope remained where I could see my beating Van Dam. Van Dam's weakest fishing technique is sight fishing, and it is one of my greatest strengths. I figured that if conditions got just right on Lake Champlain I might have a chance to beat him. Every so often the quality bass get in the spawning mode and are not very catchable on power type baits like spinnerbaits, crankbaits, and jigs. As a result, the sight fishermen usually dominate. This does not happen often, and I knew the chances of it happening were slim.

WHEN GOD DECIDES SOMETHING IS GOING TO HAPPEN, NO POSITIVE OR NEGATIVE VISUALIZATION IS GOING TO CHANGE HIS WILL. WHEN GOD DECIDES IT'S YOUR TIME TO WIN, YOU WIN.

The quality fish would have to be visible on their beds spawning (an ideal condition for sight fishing) and otherwise hard to catch. Even when some fish are on the beds spawning, you can still use a variety of ways to catch prespawn fish. Also, the typically blustery winds on that lake would have to calm, as it's easier to sight fish on smooth water. All these variables would have to line up in order to ensure a victory. It was a remote, outside chance, and the odds of it happening were definitely against me.

I wasn't the only one who didn't figure I had much of a chance to beat Van Dam. The whole bass fishing industry considered it a foregone conclusion—Van Dam would easily wrap up his second consecutive AOY title on Lake Champlain. I only talked to one person who thought I had a chance. Fellow Skeeter Team pro, Dean Rojas, was the only guy in the world, it seemed, who thought I could beat Van Dam. Dean even tried to give me a pep talk one day at Lake Fork before we left for New York, but I wasn't too receptive.

WHEN THE TOURNAMENT ROLLED AROUND, THINGS TOOK A TURN FOR THE BETTER. THE CONDITIONS WERE EXACTLY LIKE I HAD HOPED.

Even so, when the tournament rolled around, things took a turn for the better. The conditions were exactly like I had hoped. The first two days were bright and sunny with absolutely no wind, not a ripple on that huge lake. Indeed, the quality fish were on the beds spawning, and they were otherwise hard to catch. On the first day of the tournament, I had 16 pounds of smallmouth bass and was in about twentieth place—about ten places ahead of Van Dam who was around thirtieth place with 14 pounds. A twinkle came to my eye when I realized I had a chance. I needed to step it up, though, because I needed to beat him by twenty-nine places to win.

Again on the second day, not a breath of wind blew across Lake Champlain—very unusual indeed. I had 17 pounds of smallmouth bass, and I moved up to sixth place. Van Dam shocked everyone with only 13 pounds, and he fell to forty-fourth place. I had him by 38 points, but it wasn't over yet. The fact that I was in sixth place after Day Two meant nothing. On the FLW Tour in 2002, they cut the field to the top twenty after two days of competition. All top twenty fishermen start over at zero points for the third day. Even though Van Dam had been cut from the field, I still had to go out and fish the third day, finishing fifteenth or better out of the top twenty fishermen to win AOY. I had to fish one more day, and I had to beat at least five of the remaining twenty guys to win the title.

And what a struggle that third day turned out to be! I only had about 10 pounds when I headed for weigh-in, unsure whether that would be enough to pull off the win. I arrived five minutes early and pulled up on the point right outside check-in. Two boats were already fishing the point, including my friend, Tommy Biffle. I pulled up outside Tommy, way out off the point to be sure I wasn't in his way, and dropped a Berkley tube into 20 feet of water. I looked at my watch—four minutes until check-in. When my tube hit bottom, I twitched it once and felt a bite. Soon I landed my biggest bass of the day, a 3 1/2-pound smallmouth. I culled through my limit of smallmouth bass keeping the larger fish and never even had time for another cast. It was time to go in. That last-minute bass bumped me up to 12 1/2-pounds for the day. I finished tenth that day out of twenty guys and went home with the title!

I LOOKED AT MY WATCH—FOUR MINUTES UNTIL CHECK-IN. WHEN MY TUBE HIT BOTTOM, I TWITCHED IT ONCE AND FELT A BITE. SOON I LANDED MY BIGGEST BASS OF THE DAY.

I have often wondered if that final bass won the AOY title for me. I had not weighed my fish that day on the water, so I can't be sure. I think I would have won AOY by 1 point without that final bass, but I will never know for sure. Who knows? We may have tied if I hadn't caught that final bass. Let's just say God knew what I needed to win, and He just wanted to make sure I had enough weight in my bag. I think He gave me that last big one just in case!

Although I was thrilled to win FLW Angler of the Year for a number of reasons, the best part about the win was the fact that I would now be featured on the cover of Kellogg's Corn Flakes cereal boxes at all the Wal-Marts across America. God knows what He is doing. Gracing the cover of a cereal box does a ton for your credibility, which, in turn, gives you more opportunities to share the gospel. The celebration over the AOY win, however, was short-lived. According to the official schedule, the six-day practice period for the BASSMASTERS Classic on Lay Lake in Alabama fell immediately after the FLW season finale in New York. In fact, after staying over in New York an extra day to do the photo shoot for the Corn Flakes box for Kellogg's, I loaded the family up in my Chevy Suburban and drove nearly straight through to Birmingham, Alabama arriving a day late.

Daddy, don't worry.
God just told me you are going to win the Classic.

—My daughter, Hannah Yelas, the night before
the final day of the 2002 BASSMASTERS Classic.

Chapter Nine

A CLASSIC FINISH

Since I arrived in Birmingham a day late, I missed a day of the six-day practice period. I wasn't too worried. After fishing the last eleven consecutive Classics without ever contending for the win, I had made up my mind to approach this year's Classic differently and only fish one section of the lake. I didn't need six days for my new strategy of learning one small area of the lake. In my previous eleven Classics, I had always spent my six-day practice period checking out the whole lake, in an attempt to find the best water to fish. This time that wouldn't be necessary.

It was time for a change. I had nothing to lose. I was already 0-for-11 in the Classic. What would being 0-for-12 hurt? I would choose one section of Lay Lake and spend my whole practice period in that one area. I figured I might gain an advantage by learning every nook and cranny of that part of the lake. That way, if this part of the lake was "on" in the Classic, I would stand a good chance of winning. On the other hand, if it was "off," then I'd just have a good time and try again next year. It was a guess, a gamble, but I thought it just might pay off.

Courage

It took me eleven years to realize that practicing the whole lake was the wrong approach for me. Once the actual Classic starts, you can't fish the entire lake. You decide on the area you like, and that is where you fish the tournament. I realized I was wasting most of my practice days using this approach. In the past, I spent one day fishing in each of six different areas: A, B, C, D, E and F. However, if I happened to like area B the best, I would decide to fish the tournament there. When the actual tournament started, I realized I was entering the competition with only one day, or at best two days, of practice on the water I had chosen.

I have learned the hard way that one day is not enough time for me to learn an area. There is no way, with my fishing style, that I can learn an area well enough in one day to compete on it for three days during the Classic. In hindsight, for the last eleven years I had wasted the majority of my six-day practice period fishing in areas I would never go back to in the Classic.

It reminded me of a similar strategy homerun hitters use in baseball. Many times, a slugger will guess what pitch the pitcher will throw and where he will throw it. A hitter may, for example, guess "fastball on the inside corner." If he guesses right, gets his pitch, and executes, he hits a home run. If he guesses wrong, he will most likely strike out. Drawing on my baseball knowledge, I guessed "upper portion of Lay Lake, the last five miles before Logan Martin Dam." I went into this year's Classic looking for the home run ball.

I CHOSE THIS AREA BECAUSE IT HAD TWO OF THE INGREDIENTS I BELIEVE NECESSARY TO WIN A CLASSIC: THE PRESENCE OF BIG BASS AND RELATIVELY LIGHT FISHING PRESSURE.

I had fished this section of Lay Lake some during the 1996 Classic where I finished seventh. What's more, I never saw another contestant up there during the 1996 Classic. On the last day of that Classic, I ran all the way up the river and caught two bass that day that weighed almost 8 pounds; so I knew the area held big bass. A couple of my buddies who live in Alabama confirmed my belief that there were some big bass that lived in the river portion of Lay. Most of the local anglers on Lay favor the middle and lower sections of the lake, so the river was not heavily fished and I liked that. In short, I chose this area because it had two of the ingredients I believe necessary to win a Classic: the presence of big bass and relatively light fishing pressure. I was hoping that few, if any, other Classic contestants would fish the river portion of Lay, just as they had stayed away from it in 1996.

As it turned out, my prefish for the 2002 Classic was mediocre. I had a couple of good days with stringers around 12 to 14 pounds. The fishing wasn't great, but it didn't sway my strategy. I disciplined myself to stay in that part of the lake, and I was not leaving no matter how bad the fishing was. I put in the time I needed to learn that river on Lay. One of the things I discovered was the role the dam played in my fishing. The Alabama Power Company makes hydroelectric power from the dams along the Coosa River in Alabama. When they start making power, they release a lot of water from the dams, which creates tremendous currents in the river. The fish that live just below these dams change locations all day long as the currents ebb and flow. I needed to invest a lot of time up this river to figure them out during the changing currents.

THE FISHING WASN'T GREAT, BUT IT DIDN'T SWAY MY STRATEGY. I DISCIPLINED MYSELF TO STAY IN THAT PART OF THE LAKE, AND I WAS NOT LEAVING NO MATTER HOW BAD THE FISHING WAS.

Fortunately, this wasn't the first time I'd seen this kind of dynamic. I had fished many previous tournaments along the various lakes on the Coosa River in Alabama, and my past experience on these river lakes paid off. In past years, I would always run up the river during one day of practice to check things out. I would get on some fish when the dam was generating a certain current and then come back a couple of days later in the tournament to fish. Invariably, the current would be totally different the day of the tournament, and the fish would be gone. The dynamics of these "tailrace" fisheries, the fishable water just below a dam, change every hour. During the 2002 Classic prefish, I was interested in just camping out for a few days below Logan Martin Dam and figuring out those tailrace fish on Lay Lake.

After fifteen years as a pro, I was surprised to learn that the key to my success was releasing my pride.

Building Momentum

Mentoring

I felt great as I practiced for the Classic on Lay Lake. I could feel the momentum begin to surge. My great friend and spiritual mentor from Tyler, Jerry Phelps, joined me in Alabama for those five days of fishing on Lay Lake. Jerry kept saying positive things to me all week, encouraging my momentum.

Momentum is such a huge factor in any sport. The person or team with the momentum has a decided advantage. Momentum is a combination of variables, part mental and part spiritual. We can't control when momentum comes, it just happens. However, we can acknowledge its presence when it comes, thus encouraging it to stay around awhile. I sure like it when the "mo" is on my side. It's a good feeling. Even though I can't control momentum, after fifteen years as a pro, I know when I have it and when I don't. And I had it on Lay Lake as I prepared for the Classic.

When the Classic prefish concluded, Jerry and I headed for Texas, and I was ready to spend a few days at home. I felt good, even though my prefish was only mediocre. But that's what momentum does to you. It makes you feel like something good is going to happen. You can feel things going your way. In fact, this surge of momentum was a new experience. I was right in the middle of the strongest wave of momentum of my entire career, but I was not fully aware of it at the time because I did not recognize it for what it was. In retrospect, I believe what I was feeling was God's anointing. He had predestined me to win the World Championship.

The Classic was still three weeks away. For the past eleven years, I had fished quite a bit during the Classic off-limits period. I always wanted to stay on top of my game and be at my best for the World championship. Once again, 2002 would be different. I felt so good about my fishing, and I was in such a groove mentally, that I was scared to go fishing for fear of losing my momentum and/or my anointing. For the first time in my career, I never touched a rod for three weeks as I prepared for the Classic.

THAT'S WHAT MOMENTUM DOES TO YOU. IT MAKES YOU FEEL LIKE SOMETHING GOOD IS GOING TO HAPPEN. YOU CAN FEEL THINGS GOING YOUR WAY.

When Jill, the girls, and I arrived in Birmingham three weeks later for the tournament. I could feel the presence of the Holy Spirit so strong all week. When I walked into the boat yard to put away my gear, I could feel a "glow" from my boat. I didn't realize what it was at first, but I could feel a unique spiritual presence around my boat all week as it sat in the boatyard among the fifty-two other Classic boats. By midweek, I figured out what that special glow was. God had even anointed my boat!

That wasn't my first indication that something was in the works in the spiritual realm.

About three months before the Classic, I had what some might call a vision—totally out of the blue. One day as I was driving down the interstate, I had this vision that I was sitting in my boat in the Birmingham-Jefferson Civic Center parking lot waiting to weigh my stringer of fish in the 2002 Classic. I sensed I had a stringer of fish that weighed in the teens. I had never weighed a five fish stringer in the teens during the

Classic. It was just a brief picture of the future, and I didn't know what to make of it. It sure felt real though, and I had never before experienced anything like it.

Then my great friend, Mike Auten, called me about two weeks before the Classic and told me about a dream his wife, Becky, had the night before. She had dreamed I had won the Classic! Then he said Becky had dreamed the same exact dream last year about Kevin Van Dam. Two weeks later, he won the 2001 Classic! Now this was getting strange. Too many unusual things were beginning to line up. As it turns out, I believe God had already predestined me to win the 2002 Classic. It was finished in the spirit realm; it just was waiting to take place in the physical world.

Unstoppable

I could feel this surge of momentum like a tidal wave when the actual Classic competition began. I could do no wrong all week at the Classic. I caught the big bass every day of the tournament, an unprecedented feat in BASSMASTER history. I found my key spot on Tuesday, the one official practice day. A month before during the prefish, the bank had nothing but big stripers on it. In fact, there were so many stripers and shad on this bank back in June that I fished it three different days looking for, but never finding, the first bass. I checked it one last time on Tuesday, the one practice day immediately prior to competition, and caught two big spotted bass and saw a live bait fisherman catch a big bass. The best part was the school of stripers was gone. It appeared as though a big school of bass had moved in.

Because of the time I spent prefishing one location, I had also finally figured out the dynamics with the water generating from the dam. Every day the Alabama Power Company would generate water from Logan Martin Dam from 10:00 a.m. until 3:00 p.m. I was fishing 500 yards below the dam on the last good ambush points heading upriver before the dam. When they turned the water on, it would rise 3 feet, and the fish would predictably move up to the shallow banks and hang out in little shade pockets, in front of undercut banks, ambushing shad.

A spotted-bass keeper during the 2002 Classic on the last day.

On the first day of the Classic, I caught a 4 1/2-pound spotted bass from under an overhanging tree. As I fished on up the bank, a boat with three old men pulled right up to where I had just caught that big fish and dropped anchor. All three men tossed live shad under the tree where I had just caught the big bass. I fished on up the bank a ways, then turned around and headed back towards them. As I got close, I heard them say, "Let's go. They're not here today." They pulled anchor and left. Five minutes later, I tossed my jig under the same tree and caught the big bass of the day, a 6-pound, 2-ounce beauty. That bass had been looking at live shad for thirty minutes, but the Lord kept that fish's mouth shut until I came along to scoop her up. Later the same day, I headed back to weigh-in about ten minutes early just

Holding the biggest bass of the 2002 Classic (6 pounds, 4 ounces) and a smaller spotted bass.

to be safe. After my 30-mile run back, I had a few minutes left, so I just pulled up to a nearby dock, flipped in, and yanked out a three and a half pound spotted bass! It was the first dock I had fished all day.

I PAUSED, THEN SAID, "IT WOULD TAKE AN ACT OF GOD TO CATCH ONE NOW!" ON MY VERY NEXT FLIP, I CAUGHT A 6-POUND, 4-OUNCE GIANT.

On the second day, the Lord's hand was even stronger! Late in the day, I had about 11 pounds that I'd caught on Berkley jigs and Frenzy® crankbaits. I was fishing up my best bank, while a pontoon boat with live shad fishermen drifted towards me, catching bass as they drifted. When they got down to where I was, I figured out they were apparently upset at me (and my entourage of forty boats) for invading their fishing hole. They fired up their motor right next to my boat and put the hammer down. The right side of their boat was nearly touching the over hanging trees I was fishing as they ran back upstream! I turned around to my cameraman, laughed, and said, "How am I supposed to win the Classic when people are doing stuff like that to me?" I paused, then said, "It would take an act of God for me to catch one now!" On my very next flip, I caught a 6-pound, 4-ounce giant—the biggest bass of the whole tournament! I gave the Lord an opportunity to show his power in front of an international audience on ESPN, and he gave me the biggest bass of the 2002 Classic!

CLASSICS ARE

USUALLY WON OR

LOST BY MERE

My miracle fish on Day Two reminded me of a miracle Jesus performed by turning the water to wine at a wedding party (Luke 2:1–11). His miracle did not produce just any wine, the host of the party said it was the "best" wine. My miracle fish was not just any fish, either; it was the "best" and biggest

OUNCES. THAT

LAST DAY

HELD MANY

DISTRACTIONS.

fish of the whole 2002 Classic! That's our God for you! That miracle bass gave me close to a 10-pound lead going into the third and final day of the Classic.

The Final Day

The night before the final day, my oldest daughter Hannah, then age six, woke up around 10 p.m. just as I was getting ready to go to bed. She sat up in bed, turned to me with a big smile and said, "Daddy, don't worry. God just told me you are going to win the Classic." Some guys have trouble sleeping the night before the last day of a tournament. But with her words in my mind, I drifted right off into peaceful sleep.

The main thing on my mind the next morning was how I didn't want to blow this opportunity of a lifetime. Classics are usually won or lost by mere ounces, and I had a nearly 10-pound lead going into the final day. That last day held many distractions. For starters, a writer rode along with me on the hour-long drive to the lake that morning from the hotel in Birmingham. He stuck a tape recorder in my face and interviewed me the whole hour. When I arrived at the lake, no fewer than ten reporters were waiting for me, cameras rolling, trying to get quick pre-

Focus

game interviews with me before I hit the water. As I launched my Skeeter, cranked my Yamaha, and idled out to the take-off area, I noticed at least fifty local spectator boats and an ESPN helicopter waiting to follow me up the river to watch me fish.

As I MADE THE 30-MILE RUN UPRIVER TO MY FISHING AREA AT 70 MPH, THE HELICOPTER BUZZED NOT 100 FEET ABOVE ME, COLLECTING FOOTAGE FOR ESPN.

As I made the 30-mile run upriver to my fishing area at 70 mph, the helicopter buzzed not 100 feet above me, collecting footage for ESPN. When I arrived at my spot, another twenty local spectator boats were waiting to watch me fish. I started the day with seventy spectator boats watching me, and the helicopter crew now filming me 300 feet above my head. Was I handicapped that final morning? You bet. I am sure every bass in the area was on red alert. But, hey, at least the pilot moved that whirlybird up a couple hundred feet!

Patience

The last day started out slowly, but I had faith in my water. I was not tempted to run somewhere else when the bite slowed the final morning, one of the benefits of my disciplined strategy to stay in that area of the lake. I caught my first keeper at 10:15 a.m. that morning. My fish ended up biting the best around 11:00 a.m. once the spectators thinned, the helicopter left, and the current began from the power generation. Once again, I caught the biggest bass of the day, the bite that clinched my victory. I knew I had won it as soon as I hit the ramp at the end of the day. It was so nice not to be anxious, wondering whether I had won. I could just enjoy the afternoon and soak it all in. I was now living the dream I had worked for—being World Champion.

A week after I returned home from the Classic, some friends threw a surprise celebration party for me in Tyler. And surprised I was! Wow! What a tremendous honor to have over 120 dear friends attend the party in my honor. Not long afterwards, the city proclaimed August 8 "Jay Yelas Day" in the city of Tyler. They held a big celebration downtown where the Tyler mayor

The crowd roared and the cameras rolled as Jill, Hannah, Bethany, and I got ready to take our victory lap inside the packed Birmingham-Jefferson Civic Center.

presented me with a key to the city. This was also a tremendous honor I'll never forget.

Reflections on a World Championship

For fifteen years, I had struggled to make the pinnacle of the sport and had never quite gotten there. I never would have thought the key to making it all the way to the top revolved around releasing all my pride. Looking back, I should have known better. Ever since I had become a Christian, my fishing success paralleled my spiritual maturity. I had to learn what it meant to be a champion in life long before I was ready to be a World Champion.

I should have been able to see that pattern and search my heart for more ways to grow closer to the image of Jesus Christ. Following that logic, it looks like there is no end to what I can do with my fishing because I am still nowhere near the likeness of Jesus Christ. I am growing more like Him daily, but I still make plenty of mistakes every day.

When the day unfolds like a masterpiece—those are the days that keep us coming back for more.

However, even if I do one day become a saint, (and those who know me best say there is no chance of that happening!) there is no guarantee my fishing success will continue to grow. That part is totally up to God. If it is His will for me to win another Classic, it will happen. If He doesn't will it, I have no problem with that decision.

For me, the biggest thrill of the whole tournament was when I was able to thank Jesus for the win while live on ESPN, and talk about how He had changed my life. You see, by gracefully allowing me to win the FLW Angler of the Year and the BASSMASTERS Classic in 2002, God has already given me the platform I need to share His love with a lost and dying world. If I win a regular season tournament on one of the pro Tours next season, will it give me a bigger platform to share Jesus? Not likely. If I win a national AOY title in 2003, will that give me a bigger platform to share Jesus? Maybe. If I win the Classic again, would I have an even bigger platform to share Jesus? Yes, but not too much bigger than the one I have now.

These days, I am only interested in winning fishing titles if they can be used to benefit the kingdom of God. Worldly success gives us a platform to glorify Jesus Christ through our personal testimonies. I know what a relationship with Jesus Christ has meant to my life, and I want to see others live the abundant life as well. Encouraging others in their relationship with Jesus Christ is my reason for living; it's what drives me and brings me the most satisfaction.

I have been a very busy man for the last ten years. However, this Classic win propelled me to a whole new realm of busyness. It is almost overwhelming. I have been amazed at the magnitude and scope of the demands on my time. Everybody wants a piece of my time. I have had invitations to speak at functions ranging from fishing seminars, to churches, to schools, to bass clubs, to radio shows, to TV shows, to men's clubs, to civic groups, and even professional business conferences across the nation. I have seriously considered hiring an employee to help me with this workload! I can definitely see the value of having someone to do the things in my day that anybody could do so that I can concentrate on the things that only I can do.

Additionally, my sponsors have been working me hard to take advantage of the new opportunities. Berkley, in particular, worked with me for fifteen days between the Classic and the end of 2002, filming commercials, footage for the "Sportsmans Challenge" TV show, and an infomercial. In the months immediately following the Classic, I took on two new endorsement opportunities, including one with Chevrolet and one with Mustad. I wrote this book and even signed a deal for a bobblehead doll. I turned down an opportunity to go to Venezuela with Citgo and ESPN on a Peacock Bass fishing trip so I could finish this book. I have learned how to say "no," in order to keep my sanity.

> I KNOW WHAT A RELATIONSHIP WITH JESUS CHRIST HAS MEANT TO MY LIFE. ENCOURAGING OTHERS IN THEIR RELATIONSHIP WITH JESUS CHRIST IS MY REASON FOR LIVING; IT'S WHAT DRIVES ME AND BRINGS ME THE MOST SATISFACTION.

Worth the Wait

Patience

No wonder the Lord waited for me to mature as a Christian before putting this load on me. I am glad I was thirty-seven when my ship came in. I have come to terms with the fact that Christians play by a different set of rules when it comes to professional sports. To be sure, God loves all people the same, whether we believe in Him or not. However, I believe he takes special consideration of those who call Him, Father. He knows what we can and cannot handle. For example, a young, immature Christian may not be able to handle the fame and fortune that goes with winning Angler of the Year on a national Tour and being a World Champion. It could go to his head and puff him up with pride and ruin his testimony. So many young athletes in other sports who are blessed with fame and fortune too soon prove they are too young to handle it. That would be a tragedy, and God loves His own too much to let it happen to one of them. Therefore, He patiently waits for us to grow and mature in our faith to become more like Jesus Christ. He knows that the more we become like Jesus, the more we can handle fame and fortune without it pulling us away from Him.

THE LORD WAITED FOR ME TO MATURE AS A CHRISTIAN BEFORE PUTTING THIS LOAD ON ME. I AM GLAD I WAS THIRTY-SEVEN WHEN MY SHIP CAME IN.

I am sure glad He waited until I had matured enough as a Christian to be able to handle it. As a maturing believer, He helps me take it all in stride, knowing that He was the One who made it all happen. I take no pride in my wins of 2002. All the glory goes to Jesus Christ.

Still Loving It

We have all had days on the water where everything clicks, when we paint a masterpiece—finding some fish on our own and figuring out how to catch them the way we like to on our favorite lure or technique. When we come in at the end of a day like that, we feel a certain satisfaction that is very fulfilling. I never grow tired of this part of bass fishing. Unfortunately, not every day turns out to be a masterpiece. However, the days that do keep us coming back for more.

The best outcome from my Classic and FLW wins in 2002 will be their benefits to other people. I don't want them to be for my benefit only—but for society as a whole. I want my wins to follow Romans 8:28 and "work together for good" in order to help others. That's why I hope you received something in the pages of my book. If you did, then God has accomplished His goal. My success in 2002 was just for you.

Oh what a wonderful god we have!
How great are his riches and wisdom and knowledge!
For everything comes from him,
everything exists by his power and is intended for his Glory.
To him be Glory evermore, Amen.

—Romans 11:33, 36 (NLT)

AFTERWORD

What I Mean by "Holy Spirit"

In a further effort to explain being spirit led while I fish, I believe more of an explanation on communicating with God in the workplace is necessary. This is not an easy communication process to pick up and requires a lot of discernment and faith. Early on, I had a hard time discerning if that voice in my head was the Holy Spirit or if it was just my intellect. I admit that it was confusing at first. Building a relationship with God, getting to know how He works, and incorporating Him into our workplace takes time. However, I eventually learned an important distinction between the voice of the Holy Spirit and my intellect. The Holy Spirit, as an expression of God's personality, is never wrong; but my intellect is often wrong. The key to telling the two apart is to determine if the idea you are hearing in your head is something new and original or if it stems from something you have experienced before. If it is something new, it is more than likely from the Holy Spirit. All your intellect knows is what it has experienced.

The presence and activity of the Holy Spirit in my fishing is electric and so very exciting. It quickens my inner man—the core of who I am. I used to think that I experienced this gleeful sensation because of something I had done. Perhaps I had discovered something unique about the fish that the other contestants had not, or maybe I had found a neat angle on how to catch them everyone else had overlooked. At least that's what it seemed to be as I looked at life from the natural realm. Yet I soon discovered that the special feeling I had when I found some good fish was the presence of the Holy Spirit. I was experiencing an anointing from the Lord to be used for His glory and service. Now that's exciting! It has nothing to do with the other contestants, or the bass, or anything that I have figured out on my own. In fact, this "anointing" (or presence of the Holy Spirit) does not originate in us; it is God's gift to us. He lends it to us for His service.

How do we receive this gift? We cannot receive God's anointing unless we are in right relationship with the Lord. Repentance from ungodly attitudes and actions is a must. Additionally, if we want the Holy Spirit's presence, we must keep our hearts pure before God. The Bible says, "Blessed are the pure in heart, for they will see God" (Matthew 5:8). I must be broken and humble before God in order to experience Him. This does not mean that I must only appear to others to be a humble, godly man. God sees what is in my heart, not what's on the outside. You can appear outwardly humble while remaining inwardly pompous if you are a good actor.

Finally, we cannot want God's anointing just to increase our performance for our own benefit. That's not it at all. It must be for the benefit of others. I want the Holy Spirit to command my fishing so that I can do my best for Him and bring Him glory. Only then can He can use me to touch other people's lives. Tournament wins are just one of many ways He can use me to help build His kingdom. You see, God attaches great responsibility to this gift. Jesus Himself reminded us that to whom much is given, much is required (Luke 12:48).

Once you discern the Holy Spirit's voice, you then must have the faith to believe it is true and the willpower to act on that faith. To me, this is the most exciting part of fishing but one of the most difficult to execute. It's exciting because it's a chance to have faith in God and not be consumed with yourself. We must cultivate our spiritual awareness at all times. Desire it, crave it, and long for it more than anything else. Then your mind and soul will be ready to obey that still, small voice of the Holy Spirit when it comes.

At the same time, the exciting part is also the hardest part: having the faith to trust that still, small voice. Done right, we must allow even one whisper from the Holy Spirit to sway a wealth of preparation, knowledge, and planning. Obedience requires faith, especially when His guidance flies in the face of all we know. The key is to have the faith and trust in Him just like a little child trusts his daddy. It is good to plan our own strategy, but when He speaks, we must immediately drop our plans and obey. Indeed, faith and obedience, the two pillars of the Christian faith, are also the keys to world class performances in the workplace.